Something

of the

Turtle

Something

of the

Turtle

Sandra Clayton

To purchase additional copies of this book please call 888-934-0888 or
go to www.wheatmark.com/bookstore

Something of the Turtle

Published by Wheatmark®
610 East Delano Street, Suite 104
Tucson, Arizona 85705 U.S.A.
www.wheatmark.com

International Standard Book Number: 978-1-60494-066-4
Library of Congress Control Number: 2008930031

Contents

Gibraltar

The Atlantic Ocean

The Madeira Islands

About Voyager

Voyager is a heavy cruising catamaran built by Solaris Yachts in Southampton, England. They produced strong, very comfortable boats but sadly they are no longer in business. Voyager is their *Sunstream* model, 40 ft long x 16 ft wide with twin 27hp diesel engines.

Her two hulls are connected by a bridge deck with a cabin on it which provides the main living area, or saloon. It contains a large sofa, a dining table and a chart table for navigation work.

From the saloon, you enter the starboard or right-hand hull down three steps. Immediately in front of you is the galley. Turn right, and in the stern is a double bed. Underneath is one of her engines. At the bow end of this hull is a head, or bathroom, which does actually contain a bath.

The port hull contains another double bed in the stern, also with a diesel engine under it. There is a further cabin and bed in the bow of this hull but for the voyage we converted it into storage space with a small bench and vise.

Out on deck she has a deep, well protected cockpit and all her sails can be handled within it.

Warning - Disclaimer

This book is a personal memoir written to entertain the reader with the Clayton's own sailing experiences. Any descriptions or comments made about boats, sailing or seamanship are included only to offer the reader a fuller experience of their life at sea. Under no circumstances are any of the descriptions or comments included in this book intended, nor should they be considered as intended, as offering advice on sailing or encouragement to take up sailing in any of its many forms. Sailing can be dangerous and should not be undertaken without professional training and supervision until an appropriate level of competence is reached.

Nor is this book offering advice or encouragement on retirement options or on early retirement. These were choices made by the author and her husband who were fully aware of the physical and financial risks which are considerable.

None of the descriptions or comments in this book is intended as a recommendation of any of the places visited. Names of people, boats and the make and types of boats have been changed to protect the individual's privacy.

Note on the Text

In Britain, and much of Europe, wind and vessel speeds are described in knots. One knot equals a nautical mile covered in one hour and is roughly equivalent to 1.15mph. Also used is the Beaufort Wind Force Scale.

For the reader's convenience, however, I have used miles per hour in this book in place of knots, although I have retained the occasional reference to the Beaufort Scale. For example, *Strong Gale Force 9* carries far more associations and implications for the seagoing than a simple wind speed of 47-54mph. It also provides a flavour of European sailing.

For similar reasons of local color I have not changed currencies to US dollars. At the time of these events, the currency exchange was roughly $US1.50 to £1sterling. Europe had not yet converted to the Euro and still retained its individual currencies.

Overview

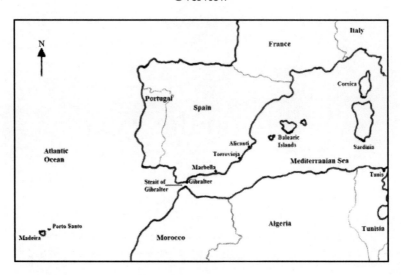

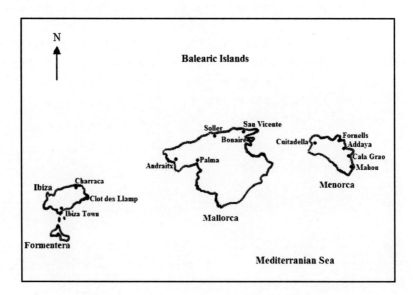

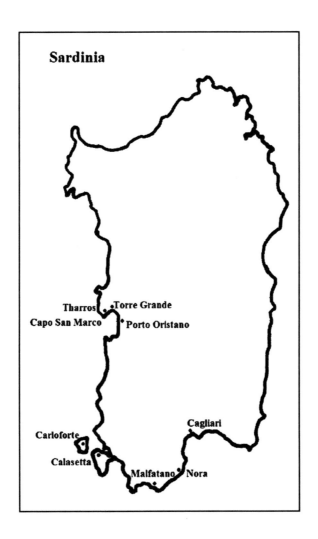

Sardinia

Tharros
Torre Grande
Capo San Marco
Porto Oristano

Carloforte
Cagliari
Calasetta
Malfatano
Nora

England

1

Selling Up

....

It is only when you come to sell up your home that you truly understand the nature of consumerism. It means that while you pay through the nose for your goods and chattels, when you come to sell them a dealer will offer next to nothing for the entire houseful. You cannot give electrical goods to charity shops because it costs them too much to get them certified safe before they can risk re-selling them to their customers. Nor can they accept upholstered furniture beyond a certain age, because of new Health & Safety regulations regarding fire hazard. Putting everything into store is not a viable option either, since over a period of time you will pay in storage fees and insurance charges many times their replacement value. And, when you do finally get them back, your couch will look shabbier than you remembered and nobody will carry spare parts for your electrical goods any more.

We decide, therefore, to store only those things which really mean something to us. That means certain pieces of furniture and personal items. The furniture isn't a problem; a desk each, a dining set, a chest of drawers and Grandma's old dresser. Things like beds, bedroom furniture, lounge suites and bookcases are best replaced when the time comes.

Some personal effects are equally easy to decide on. The easiest of all are the photo albums. Photographs are your life in pictures: snapshots of moments in time; special places; people and animals you love; and your own face looking back at you, like Rembrandt's self-portraits with their silent questions about life, happiness, mutability and mortality.

One couple who came to view our house had put all their possessions in store and the storage facility had burnt down. They were fully

3

reimbursed by the insurance company but said that some things were irreplaceable, particularly photographs of family and friends, their life together and especially the children growing up. With their experience in mind, we decide we will still put our albums into store with our other belongings, but leave the negatives with David's brother Tony, just in case.

WITH THE ESSENTIALS DECIDED on, there remains a huge balance to be disposed of which presents a very great difficulty. Not for David, of course. When we married his belongings barely filled a small suitcase and more than three decades later there is not much more that he wants to keep. But for me it is a task bordering on the Herculean. Where do I start?

With the genes, I'm afraid, for I am the child of an Olympic-standard hoarder. My Mom filled the family home to capacity. Open a drawer and you skinned your knuckles trying to flatten the contents sufficiently to close it again. Open a cupboard and everything toppled forward to meet you. The clothes in her wardrobe had to be shoulder-charged to get the door shut. The wrists of a Samson were required to extract the big bread-and-butter plate from under fifteen other plates of descending size in a towering pyramid that lurched at you as you struggled to slide out the one Mom wanted. As a newly-wed I swore I would never let my own home get the same.

When my mother died aged 85 her house was filled to the rafters. I still have thirty years to go but my own house is already as full, including many of my parents' things because when the time came I simply could not bring myself to dispose of them. Not always because I particularly liked them, but because they were theirs and also because many of them had been part of my life ever since my eyes first began to focus. By nature, nurture and natural inclination, then, I am a hoarder.

My problem now falls into two basic categories. These can most usefully be labeled *Me* and *Significant Others*.

With regard to the former, it feels as if it is me that is being disposed of; as if the house is being emptied because I have died. This is, after all, something other people usually do for you after you've gone. And being still alive, in a culture where an individual is defined largely by possessions, there is a sense in which I will cease to exist without them. Our cupboards and wardrobes contain the history of my life in *things*.

The ice skates, bronze medal in ballroom dancing, tennis racket—and the ancient, bulky transistor radio on which I listened to Radio Luxemburg every night under the bedclothes so that my parents wouldn't hear—are from my teenage years.

The crash helmet, horse riding helmet and boots, walking boots, bicycle and the camping equipment chart our early marriage, along with remnants of our first dinner service—and our second, for after 34 years we are on our third. Both the earlier sets had come with promises that you would be able to buy additions and replacements in perpetuity; but one disappeared off the market soon after we bought the basics, and the other changed color so dramatically that there was no point anyway.

There is a book of English madrigals from a summer school; a metronome, all that remains of my attempt at learning classical guitar; a notebook of alphabet music for playing steel pans that immediately brings to mind the joy of making music with other people but without worrying about musical theory. There are dressmaking patterns, corn dollies, theatre programs, old letters and greeting cards, pictures we don't hang any more but which witnessed such happy times, and two cardboard suitcases we bought in a department store in 1964, as indigent newly-married 20-year-olds to carry our worldly goods to Australia on our first big adventure together and now, 34 years later, we have embarked on another.

The second area of difficulty is all those things which, by gift or inheritance, have come from people who have been important in my life. These things I can't even begin to think about.

I therefore decide to start with the easiest. The wardrobes.

2

Setting Out

The previous summer David and I had set off from England in our
40-foot catamaran, Voyager. The *plan* was to sail her to the Mediterranean for the winter and then, depending how we got on, to head for the
Caribbean the following year. The *hope* was that a warmer, drier climate
would improve our health and quality of life.

Our bid to achieve this major life-change via a boat took family and
friends by surprise since none of them sailed and, until quite recently,
neither had we. A number of factors were involved in the decision. In
particular, despite our desperate need to escape from northern cold and
damp, neither of us has the right kind of skin for prolonged exposure to
the sun. At the same time, we wanted to be physically active in the open
air, since much of our working life had been spent sitting in offices and
cars. Somewhere in the equation had been David's late-flowering interest
in sailing, and a particularly rain-sodden Sunday when he had said bleakly,
'I want another adventure before I die' which was the closest I ever heard
him get to a mid-life crisis. And whilst we loved visiting foreign places,
there is little pleasure to be had in budget air travel and hotels. A boat
enabled us to travel independently, be physically active out of doors and
take our home comforts and all necessary shade with us.

The route we had chosen was down the Atlantic coasts of France,
Spain and Portugal. However, given the dangers from autumn gales along
this coastline we had been eager to have our boat safely in the Mediterranean by the end of September. Despite our departure having to be delayed
until August, when David was hospitalized, we nevertheless achieved our
goal.

By the beginning of November—fitter and more relaxed than we had been in many years—we were happily berthed in the idyllic harbor of Mahon, capital of the beautiful Balearic island of Menorca. The only cloud on our horizon since setting out had been our house back in England. Unwaged and pre-pension, we could not afford to go blue water cruising *and* keep the house, which had been up for sale since early spring.

In the past, whenever we had wanted to sell a house, the market in our area of the country had invariably gone into a long decline. Now was no exception. But at the end of October we had received an offer. Not a good one, but the fact that it was a cash offer was an incentive to accept it. A man and a woman, both divorced and with two children each, had formed a new family. Both had had homes up for sale, but the man's had now been sold and contracts were about to be exchanged on the woman's. They also wanted to move into our house in time for Christmas which was just two months away.

Combined with a cash offer, the speed of completion persuaded us to accept the rather disappointing purchase price because it meant that in only a few weeks' time we should be relieved of the burden of household heating and maintenance costs, insurance premiums, utility bills and local taxes, all of which were currently a large drain on our limited resources. And of course the purchase money, once invested, would give us an income to live on.

In the meantime we had found a safe berth for Voyager for the short time we should be away. It also happened to be on the delightful waterfront of a charming town on a beautiful island. And although the tourists had all gone for the winter and the yachts in the harbor all lay empty, the sun still shone, the sky was bright blue and summer flowers continued to bloom.

So, there we were, with this little piece of earthly paradise all to ourselves and every expectation of a quick house sale. All we needed now was for our purchasers to get a survey done and sign a contract of sale. Then we should take a short flight back to England, exchange contracts, empty the house, hand over the keys and catch a flight back to Menorca for a warm Christmas and a nice bit of winter sailing.

If only life was that simple.

3

Sorting Out

There are clothes I simply won't need in our new life; some I haven't worn in years anyway. I spread the contents of a wardrobe over the bed. The problem is that they aren't just clothes. They are tangible memories of a past that can never be repeated: special occasions, family weddings, anniversaries; clothes I have adored, clothes I have put a huge effort into making and woolens my mother knitted with love. And then there are the shoes, of course. I mull over it all for an hour and then put everything back into the wardrobe again, grateful that it is time to go and cook dinner and I can put off any decisions for another day.

After a second abortive attempt I give up wardrobes and empty a cupboard instead, expecting that this will be easier. I take out the contents and spread them around the floor until there is only room to tiptoe delicately between them with the precision of a performer in a Japanese Noh play.

I pick up the items one-by-one. This is from my earliest childhood; this was given to me by an incredibly kind neighbor. This was my Dad's, my Mom's, my grandparents'; these were gifts from family, friends, a teacher, and David's lovely, giggly little Grandma. David brought this home when we were first married; this was my coming-of-age present from my parents; here are the 78rpm records my Dad used to play and my drawing exercises from night school. And over there is the brass bowl that resulted from the metalwork option at day-continuation college during my first year at work. Looking at it I can still smell the metal filings, hot from the grinder. Everything I touch conjures up a loved person, a happy moment, a small achievement.

Another day, another cupboard. Here are all the gadgets you buy in a lifetime, use only briefly, but never throw away because they might come in useful one day and, irrelevantly, because of the length of time you've already held on to them and because of what they originally cost. All the things you bought when you were young in the unquestioning name of novelty; or later, tempted by promises that they would make life easier or meals tastier and healthier. And so I unwrap the electric frying pan that never did what they claimed it would, the fondue set that produced monotonous meals and singed fingers in equal proportions, and the juice extractor so cumbersome that it took longer to dismantle and clean after use than it did for somebody to grow the oranges in the first place.

Then there is the mountain of tapes, set books and course notes which after seven angst-ridden, blissful, book-throwing, life-enhancing years of part-time study had resulted in an Open University degree. There are the dog leads, brushes and combs that were once the daily accompaniments of a life made joyous by two rough collies—or *Lassie dogs* as people called them, from those old films and television series. On our walks they got so used to the cry of 'Lassie!' from approaching strangers that they would automatically stop, wag their tails and stand to be patted.

There is also the pottery collection. No holiday had ever been complete without a ceramic pot. I remember a newspaper article some years ago about a family whose mother had become one of the many people who disappear inexplicably from home every year. A married son said that she had always looked after the family very well and had seemed happy enough. She had a dresser, he said, with a row of blue china ornaments across the top and every six months she took them down, washed them, put them away and replaced them with yellow china ornaments. I look at the dusty row of brown pots along the top of my kitchen dresser and wonder where she is now and if she is happy.

I abandon the cupboards and make a start on the bookcases. Feng shui warns against a full bookcase. If it is full, goes the philosophy, there is no room for anything new in your life. My bookcases are groaning. You couldn't force in even the slimmest new volume let alone a new life.

There are books from early childhood, prizes from school and night classes and ten volumes of the second-hand encyclopedia I bought with one of my first pay packets but which were hopelessly out of date even then. There are also the books that had belonged to David's grandfather. Although he had died before David and I met, I always felt I knew him from his books. He was an active reader and the margins are full of his thoughts.

Like the wardrobes and cupboards, my books chart my life history: interests, fads and pleasures plus a lifetime's craving to find answers to all those questions beginning with 'Why…' Many have not been read in years because I have been too tired at the end of a working day, and after cooking dinner have put my feet up in front of the television instead. And if truth be told I have moved on from most of my books while finding it impossible to let them go. The ones that still have something to say to me, and which I really want to read again, are already on board Voyager.

At least I have plenty of time for this mooch down Memory Lane, thanks to our purchasers.

4

Lovely Mahon

If, by the time we had got Voyager safely berthed, our purchasers had made arrangements for a survey to be done we should undoubtedly have taken the first available flight home and set about emptying our house. But they hadn't. Unlike the property markets in some other parts of the world, English conveyancing is untrammeled by the concept of due diligence, where the purchaser's deposit is lost if an agreed deadline is not met. In England a man's word is his bond, so the laying out of hard cash on a surveyor's report is the first concrete evidence of serious intent. In its absence, doubt had emerged, and we had decided to remain where we were until a survey had been done and there was some sign of a contract about to be signed.

We had chosen Mahon after consulting a list of places recommended by yachtsmen who had wintered in the Mediterranean before us. We could not have made a happier choice. At 26 miles long by 11 miles wide, Menorca is the second-largest of the Balearic Islands lying some 50 miles off Spain's southern coast. Mahon harbor is sheltered, our berth was secure and our surroundings were truly beautiful. An additional bonus would prove, over time, to be the marina manager, Joss.

Mahon was not simply a beautiful place to wait while the initial formalities of our house sale were completed. The Mediterranean climate was having a beneficial effect on both of us and especially on David's respiratory system. Back home in England the cold and damp of winter had already settled in, while Menorca's November temperatures—comparable to an English high summer—allowed us to continue sailing or to roam on foot or bicycle. The island is a place of pretty villages and lovely beaches;

its capital a harmonious mix of white-walled cottages, grand mansions, and small market gardens bordered by dry-stone walls with gates made from twisted olive branches. And on our rambles we could rest under trees still heavy with ripe oranges or sit in a sunlit square, with coffee and an English newspaper.

Two weeks passed and our purchasers had still not arranged for a survey. For people claiming they wanted to be in before Christmas, this was troubling. Then a telephone call from the estate agent in England confirmed our suspicions. Someone had been economical with the truth. Contracts had *not* been in the process of being exchanged on the woman's house, as claimed when the 'cash offer' had been made on ours, for the simple reason that her ex-husband was refusing to sign the contract of sale. There would be no problem, we were assured, the house was part of the divorce settlement and if he refused the latest request to sign then a judge in the Family Court would sign on his behalf. It would take a couple of weeks, but everything would still go through in good time. This did at least explain the lack of urgency in getting a surveyor's report. In the meantime, we were enjoying Mahon.

After setting sail from England we had anchored out wherever possible. And keen to reach the Mediterranean before those infamous autumn gales began lashing the Atlantic coast, we had had little time to loiter along the way. Accordingly, this was the first occasion on which we had spent any time in one place and close enough inshore to be part of a neighborhood. Now, however, we were part of the fabric of a small stretch of Mahon harbor.

Behind us, on the quay, were five stucco houses with dark green window shutters and terracotta roofs, with living quarters above and businesses or garages below. The local people—including those working on the boats along the waterfront—frequented the café at one end, and bought lobster and langoustine from the seafood shop at the other. In the garages between, house owners without yards, drives or gardens, threw children's parties on Saturdays. Each weekday, on the street outside, a man with a bin welded to the front of a tricycle gathered up the brown fallen leaves from the sycamores lining the street and took them away. While northern seaside resorts become cold and gray during autumn, here the only difference between summer and winter seemed to be that the tourists had gone home and the residents had their island to themselves for a while.

Across the harbor from us lay Mahon's unexpectedly lovely naval base with its long low white buildings and manicured lawns. Every evening there, as the western sky turned red and the harbor shimmered gold, the Spanish equivalent of *Taps* or *The Last Post* echoed out across the water and the national flag was lowered.

Other sounds were less mellifluous. Around midnight on our first Sunday we both shot upright in bed, eyes staring into the darkness as all the demons of hell filled the night with their abominations. We fell back against our pillows again on realizing that it was just the dumpster on the quay being emptied. I had woken again as it started to get light, thinking a child was crying, but then remembered that sunrise is the prime time for disputes among feral cats. The striking clock on the naval base struck two minutes before the one at the church of Santa Maria above us, and four minutes before another further up in the town. It was therefore best to be sound asleep before midnight if possible, except on Sundays when the dumpsters were emptied and it made no difference anyway.

The Christmas lights started to go up in the streets and the big super-market across town began filling up with dolls in rich velvet dresses, festive tins of biscuits and some particularly delicious bars of chocolate which we began to sample quite heavily, especially the truffle. I suspected we were putting on weight but the bathroom scales seemed to have disappeared.

I began making plans for Christmas dinner on board. The logistics of the usual roast turkey—with three different stuffings (sage and onion, chestnut and sausage), roast potatoes with three other types of vegeta-bles and a thickened gravy, plus steamed Christmas pudding and brandy sauce—all jockeying for space among two gas rings and an oven the size of a shoebox, would need a little planning. The first agreed compromise was going to be the turkey. It would have to be a small chicken. The rest had still to be negotiated.

IN THE SECOND WEEK of December we heard from the estate agent again. A survey had finally been done on our house. The main fault was a bit of flashing around one chimney but on the strength of it the purchas-ers were demanding another huge reduction in the purchase price. They would also be interested in some of our rugs and furniture. David told the agent we would get back to him.

'Well?' he said, as he hung up the 'phone.

'Well,' I replied, 'that amount should cover the chimney flashing, the surveyor's report, their solicitor's costs, removal expenses and even after paying us next to nothing for our rugs and furniture out of it there should still be a little something left towards a house warming party.'

'I suppose,' David said, 'that knowing our situation they think they can take us for all they can get.'

It was the 'rugs and furniture' that had angered me most. I knew the two of them had been in the house a number of times to 'measure up', even before getting the survey done. It had not occurred to me, however, that they might be treating our home as some sort of bargain basement in which to pick up our best bits and pieces on the cheap. On the strength of their cash offer and short deadline we had dropped the price well below what we thought was fair, stopped cruising and hurried into a berth— only to spend the last six weeks like sitting ducks waiting to be plucked.

That afternoon we climbed the hill to the travel agent. Two days later we flew home. We arrived at midnight and breakfasted late. It was cold, overcast and drizzling. The northern English sky was battleship gray and the damp palpable. I was shocked at the change in David. Already his breathing was audible and he looked exhausted. He was about to dial the estate agent's number when a key turned in the lock of the front door. It opened just as I got there. Framed in the doorway was the estate agent's assistant. Behind her were our purchasers, come to do some more measuring up. One look at my face and the estate agent's assistant asked them to wait in her car.

It is good to have an opportunity to express one's feelings at full flood when you are really mad. Why develop stress-related illness when you can pass it on to the very people you are paying to save you from it in the first place? Whilst assuring the woman pressed into the corner of our couch that none of my anger was directed at her, she was left in no doubt as to my feelings towards our purchasers, or what they could expect if they set foot in our house again before contracts had been signed. She was most understanding and drove them away.

David then rang the estate agent and asked him when we could expect contracts to be signed and exchanged. There would be some delay, it now appeared, as our purchasers' purchaser had not yet completed the sale of *his* house due to delays caused by *his* purchaser.

So. It never had been a cash offer in the first place, and we were now entangled in something we had drastically reduced our house price in the expectation of avoiding—a chain. The agent was asked for his assessment of the current state of the housing market. *Dead* about summed up his response. His view was echoed by all the other For Sale boards, creaking forlornly in the wind, which we had observed from the taxi on our way home from the airport. Despite our frustration, the sensible option in the circumstances seemed to be to continue with the purchasers we had, because purchasers at present were pretty thin on the ground.

'However,' David said, 'they can whistle for any further reduction in the price and our goods aren't up for grabs.'

"I shall tell them,' the agent had said diplomatically, 'that you do not consider the requested reduction to be justified and that your belongings will be going into store.'

'Fine,' said David.

When he hung up he grinned. 'Well, there's one thing, we can have a turkey and the full works for Christmas dinner, plus central heating, unlimited use of the washing machine *and* the dish washer!'

5

Waiting to Exchange

The weeks since the offer was first made on our house have now stretched into months and all enquiries are met with obfuscation. Our house has already been kept off the market during Christmas and New Year, one of the most popular periods for home buying. And we are now well on the way to Easter and the arrival of spring, that eternal symbol of renewal and rebirth and a favorite time for people wanting to make a new start in their lives with a new home.

It takes around three weeks and a degree of detective work to discover that our purchasers are still not in a position to sign a contract of sale because their purchaser's ex-wife is refusing to hand over *his* half of the money from *their* house sale so that *he* can buy our purchasers' house.

At night I dream of doors through which Family Court judges, solicitors, estate agents, house vendors and buyers, all in the process of getting divorced from one another, go in and out like classic farce, or one of those medieval German town clocks.

During the day I agonize about the state of our boat. In the past, before every winter, we have removed all the soft furnishings, clothes, books, electrical goods and anything, in fact, which is subject to damp, mildew or mold. This winter we had left Voyager fully laden in a mild mid-December expecting to be back in about three weeks. It is now the end of February and Menorca has been undergoing one of its wettest winters ever. So has England.

Grateful at least to have been dry and warmly housed through these cold, wet months we review our situation. One of the benefits of procrastination in disposing of our goods has been a very comfortable winter.

Another is that if we need to put the house back on the market—and with the passage of time this seems increasingly likely—not only does the lived-in home look more appealing, but the sight of vendors camping out in a virtually empty house sends a message of desperation to any potential buyer.

There is, however, a wealth of surplus items which can be disposed of without detracting from the marketability of the house. For these we use auctions, newspaper advertisements, cards in the local newsagent's window and on the local supermarket's notice board, local charity shops and our first-ever car boot sale. And once the process has begun, I undergo a sea change in regard to all those personal items I have found it so difficult to discard. Suddenly the problem of the clothing and shoes becomes easy. I retain only those items I ever intend to wear again, which are very few, and accept that the rest have been kept for sentiment only. And since I have photographs of most of the occasions they represent, why hang onto them? With a sigh of relief I distribute them around the charity shops.

The photograph angle also provides a solution to the more difficult category of goods I have to address next—my lifetime in *things*. The fundamental problem appears to be that these things are Memory and that once they have gone my past has gone too. But if a sight of them is all it takes to stimulate memory, a photograph will surely do just as well as the object itself and take up far less space. So I arrange them in groups, photograph them and get rid of them.

I have loved what all these belongings represent. For the last few years, however, the things themselves have hung about me like the chains of Marley's ghost. So have those items connected with the significant others in my life. Unlike my own possessions, however, any disposal of these is imbued with guilt, for disposing of them is to somehow discard the people with whom they are associated.

But when I think this through I realize how silly this is. People do not reside in things. Those who were important to you when they were alive remain part of you after they die. You take them with you wherever you go. And it is far better to carry their positive influence with you into your future than have their memory gather dust among the bric-a-brac of your past. I like to think they would have approved of the charities to which they posthumously contributed.

WITH EASTER IMMINENT, AND still no completion in sight, we discuss the possibility of putting the house back on the market. We have had enough. Unfortunately we are painfully aware that none of the other For Sale boards in the district, many of which went up long before ours, have Sold stickers on them either. House buyers seem to have become an endangered species. Before doing anything hasty, therefore, we make discreet enquiries of another estate agent as to the current state of the market.

'I think we've seen the last of the suicides,' he says. 'And when this latest crop of bankruptcies has been dealt with I think the industry will be fitter, leaner and ready to move into the 21st century.'

We still have around nine months left of the 20th, however, and while we have no desire to spend them waiting for our 'cash' buyer to complete, we do have to be realistic. Even making allowances for the agent's gallows humor it is noticeable that a number of the most recent For Sale boards going up locally are for estate agents' own premises. The northern England property market is so dead that not only independent agencies are going out of business but even the major chains are closing branches and putting the buildings up for sale. Thanks to one of those cruel streaks of fate, the south of England is currently enjoying a much-trumpeted property boom.

Another week or two of frustration later and we decide we will put the house back on the market for Easter. Co-incidentally this is the very moment that our purchasers advise our agent that they are ready to sign a contract. However, the days go by until it is so close to Good Friday that we accept that nothing will happen now until the solicitors representing both sides return to work after the holiday. So we settle down to wait. And wait. Because after Easter our purchasers become incommunicado.

Despite the agent's best attempts to contact them, their telephone is permanently on answerphone and they do not respond to letters or people shouting through their letterbox. They cannot still be on holiday because between them they have four children in varying stages of full-time education.

Five months have now passed since the cash offer was made. After a couple of weeks of trying to get them to respond, the estate agent sends a letter to them saying that unless they get in touch within seven days the house is going back on the market. Seven days elapse. The house goes back on the market. A day or so later a couple comes to view and makes a genuine cash offer.

That same evening our original purchaser arrives on our doorstep. The situation is causing him a lot of problems, he says. He needs to move his family in as soon as possible and he would like to come in and discuss a proposition that he has for us. It had been mere chance whether David or I happened to be nearest the front door when he rang the bell. He is unlucky. He gets me. I shall draw a veil over my response but they probably heard the door slam in the next village.

DAVID ARRANGES FOR A storage company's assessor to come, emphasizing that we wish to utilize only *one* container. We take him round the house and show him the things we want to store, he makes notes and assures us they will all go in one container. Then we book two seats on a flight back to Mahon. They are very cheap, a last-minute booking on a return charter flight—far cheaper than one-way tickets—leaving the day after our goods go into store. We sell the car and have a garage sale.

The day arrives for the removal van to come with the container, pack it and take our goods away. We have put everything intended for storage together in one empty room. The two men survey it.

'Who booked this?' asks the senior of the two, sucking his teeth.

We describe the assessor.

Both men snort in unison.

'It'll never go in,' says the senior one.

It doesn't.

We are still putting stuff into piles, in the garage, for the charity shops the next morning and our neighbor very kindly volunteers to deliver them for us as we no longer have a car. We also return her spare bed, which we had borrowed overnight, having sold our own the previous day.

A friend picks us up in the afternoon to take us to the airport. It is one of those beautiful, soft sunny days you get in England in mid-May, when the trees look particularly lovely with their pale young leaves and the hawthorns across the valley are covered in white blossom.

I look at it all out of the car window as we drive away, with great pleasure but no regret. I don't live here any more. Last year, when we had left the house for the boat the first time, it had been with very mixed feelings. This second time it is with a sense of going home. Voyager is home now.

6

Flight Back to Mahon

Whenever anyone asks me to recall one of my happiest moments, I remember this day. It is pure content which is odd because I hate air travel. I hate the close confinement and I always get a 6' 7" man behind me whose restless knees grind into my pelvis for the whole journey; or two children playing a vigorous card game on the fold-down table on the back of my seat. In front I get a young woman who has bathed in perfume that morning, which makes whatever I eat or drink taste of whatever brand she is wearing for the rest of the day. Invariably she fully reclines her seat, before I have finished my meal, so that my shins are trapped and the top of her fragrant head is 6" from my nose. She will also have long hair, a strand of which she will flick rhythmically as she reclines, so that it keeps hitting me in the face.

Before we even reach these seats, however, we cause a security alert when the x-ray machine picks up a craft knife in our hand luggage. David had scooped it up with a few other useful tools prior to our garage sale. There is also a two-hour delay because our plane has not yet returned from its last flight and when it does it will have to be cleaned. And at the check-in we are 86lbs overweight on our luggage.

There are a variety of causes apart from the tools. There is the repaired, and extremely heavy, electronic control box from the automatic steering that had broken down during our arrival at Menorca; the repaired log which had been damaged by the hailstorm off Palma; a new aerial for the Navtex; replacement repair kits for the hatches that we have been promised will *definitely* fit this time; a huge roll of charts and two hefty cruising guides; not to mention a couple of items which had been overlooked when our goods had been carted off into storage and which I simply could not give away. People begin to gather round us, staring at so much luggage being taken on a week's holiday.

The very polite young man behind the desk looks at it as well, and says regretfully that he will have to charge us for excess baggage. He picks up a calculator. It is jut short of the cost of another ticket. David begins hunting through his pockets for his check book.

'We're retiring,' I say, feeling the need for some sort of justification. 'This is the last of our belongings.'

'You mean you're not going to use the return part of your ticket?' says the young man, in what seems a slightly sharper tone than earlier. Before I can do more than shake my head he says, 'Please wait a moment,' and goes to confer with his supervisor.

I look at David aghast. Oh no, me and my big mouth! Maybe you aren't supposed to do one-way trips on return flights any more. Maybe there are new rules. Maybe we'll lose our flight …

The check-in clerk comes back. 'You're definitely not returning?' he says, looking me in the eyes very earnestly.

I shake my head mournfully. It is too late to claim otherwise now, even if I wanted to.

'OK,' he says brightly. 'No charge.'

Apart from thanking him I keep my mouth firmly shut but when we are settled in the departure lounge I ask David if we are so unwanted in this land of our birth that we've been given a reward for not coming back. He laughs and says it probably has more to do with passengers bringing more weight back in, in the form of gifts and souvenirs, than they took out.

ONCE OUR 'PLANE HAS been cleaned we are allowed on board. We have the window and centre seats and there is a man sitting in the aisle seat. His two children bicker across the gangway from him while his wife, sitting beside them, looks fraught. This couple sum up everything I associate with going on holiday by air—utter misery.

Because of the long delay, the man is in sitting-down-waiting mode so instead of standing up to take off his jacket he is trying to do it while sitting in his seat. He is struggling to get his right arm out of his jacket and when he spots us approaching he goes into overdrive to get his arm free so that he can get out of his seat and let us into ours. His eyes are glazed. He has been sitting waiting in an airport for hours and his children are driving him mad; now here are people who will want to get past him and one sleeve still has an arm in it while the other is gripped by the seat somehow and rising is impossible. As we reach him he is about to tear the lining from his jacket in his desperate attempt to get free.

'Shut up, Anthony!' he snaps at the whining coming from the elder of the two boys opposite.

Beads of sweat stand out on his forehead. He is showing classic signs of stress. Our own stress has gone. Our house, that great drain on our resources, has been sold. My possessions problem, that had seemed so intractable, has been resolved and I feel all the freer for it. Our eternal goods and chattels, the ones we shall keep until we are no more or they are lost in transit, have been safely packed away and can be forgotten. Even the airline has given us an entirely unexpected going-away present. We positively float down the aisle towards the distressed man in the seat on the outside of ours.

'It's all right,' we say, unhooking his empty left sleeve from around the arm rest where it is trapping him like a straight-jacket. 'The 'plane's not going yet. Plenty of time.'

I DON'T REMEMBER IF there was a 6' 7" man with bony knees in the seat behind me. And if somebody in front reclined her seat and flicked her hair into my face I didn't notice. The noisy, boisterous children were on the other side of the aisle, and even that person who travels with me on every homeward journey, who coughs and sneezes all over me so that I'm ill with whatever virus he or she has, for at least a week after returning home, appears to have taken another flight. I don't remember ever feeling so serene, and look back upon it as a flight on angels' wings. Happiness truly is a state of mind.

The Balearic Islands

7

Mahon

After so long away from the boat we are expecting a mammoth cleaning job—mold on the inside, and her outside stained and dirty. It is the inside that had been causing us most concern, with our having left all our belongings on board for so long. In damp conditions, and with no fresh air circulating, leather goes moldy and books and clothing become musty until gradually the whole boat acquires an unpleasant smell that is impossible to get rid of. To make matters worse, some of her windows had developed leaks before we left and Menorca had experienced a lot of rain during the winter.

In the event, Voyager's inside is bone dry and mold-free thanks to Joss, the marina manager, and her decks are spotless thanks to his crew of cleaners known as The Girls. So instead of rolling up our sleeves and setting-to as expected, we open a bottle, sit in the cockpit and watch the sun go down.

It is early summer in Mahon. The sycamore trees along the quay, which were shedding brown foliage when we left, are now in green leaf, the palms up on the cliff above them are lush, and the men who empty the dumpster on the promenade shatter the silence at seven on Monday mornings now instead of Sunday midnight. And the visitors are returning. Up the quay the floating restaurants and the glass-bottomed boats are becoming busy, and the waiters from La Minerva have to dart through unaccustomed traffic to reach their sidewalk tables across the street.

The cruise ships that have spent the winter in the Caribbean are also returning, and we wander along the quay to look at them. We stand and read the data board which the crew of the four-masted Star Clipper props up on the dock. The first mast, it says, is square rigged, the other three are conventional main sails; the vessel is 336 feet long and built in 1992, the first clipper built since 1912.

Some of the conventional cruise ships that arrive are so big that when they make their left-hand turn to enter the terminal they blot out the end of the harbor completely for a time. The Saga Rose, owned by the club for the over-50s, sails past. David says, 'Crinklies,' and I say, 'You mean, our age?' Its generator vibrates through our hulls all night.

At the public quay a 120-foot private motor yacht ties up, mega-millions worth and registered in the Cayman Islands. It is so sleek at the bow, so inaccessible by external means, that the only way for the crew to clean the saloon windows is to abseil down them from the flying bridge. There are ten crew members on deck when it arrives, all in matching slacks and polo shirts—enjoying the air perhaps before the owner or his clients arrive, if Colin's experience is typical. A marine engineer we met in Wales, Colin had spent a season as crew on a luxury yacht in the Mediterranean, and found it a modern form of serfdom. Three of them had shared a windowless cabin eight feet by ten and were not allowed on deck while the family was about. 'You're bilge rats,' Colin had said with feeling.

The harbor is also busy with little boats. Among them a dinghy with two people in it and a huge brown dog filling the bow like a yeti. It sits immobile, staring ahead, taller than the humans, its fur fluttering in the breeze. After its shore leave it travels back in the same monolithic pose.

The sidewalks are abuzz, too; not least the pretty promenade edging the harbor, to where the people off the charter flights, the ferries and the cruise ships flock, and to which Voyager is tied. And thus our daily chores become part of the scene. We are street theatre. And as you peg out your smalls along the hand rails (the launderette is closed for renovation) or do your ironing in the cockpit, people by the hundred pass. It should be hell, but they have come from a long northern winter and are in holiday mood, cheerful, wry and invariably courteous.

A middle-aged man who looks as if he does hard physical work for a living, contemplates our lifestyle wistfully and says, 'Well, it's a dirty job, but I suppose somebody's got to do it.'

A little boy stares at the windmill of our wind generator and asks his Dad, 'What's it for?' Fazed for a moment, but not willing to admit defeat, the man brightens and says, 'Well, when there's no wind they use that to sail with.' Neither of them has noticed me sitting in the cockpit but the boy suddenly spots me.

'Do you?' he asks me, and the man's eyes glaze with embarrassment.

'Yes,' I say, for who am I to undermine a small boy's faith in his father?

A bluff matron says, 'Well, yerve got guts, I'll say that for yer,' which makes me wonder for a moment if she knows something I don't and whether I should quit while I'm ahead.

Although they are many, none intrude, pausing only to nod or exchange a word before moving on. For sensitivity, however, none eclipse two massive middle-aged men whose bow fronts and shaved heads suggest nightclub doormen but who have brought their elderly Mum on holiday. A tiny bird of a woman—like the genteel little landlady in the old Ealing film, *The Ladykillers*—they are walking her slowly up the quay and admiring the mainly unoccupied boats.

When they reach ours she, being tiny, does not see us sitting at our meal in the cockpit. The two men, being tall, do and both turn as one to gaze tactfully at the houses behind them. Asked a question by their mother, they turn back to answer her. As they do so she rises on tiptoe to point at whatever it is up our mast that has prompted her question and her eyes meet ours. Her face lights up.

'Ooh, look!' she chirps with delight, 'they're having their tea.'

She could not have sounded more pleased had she spotted the Queen at a royal garden party. The two huge men blush to their eyebrows and shepherd her away, while she looks back over her shoulder with sweet interest.

IF WE ARE STREET theatre, we are also a captive audience. One afternoon a boat registered in Hamburg but flying a French ensign arrives with five Frenchmen aboard. They are in their thirties except for one a decade or so older, all well-dressed and almost formal in demeanor.

After tying up they go quickly into town. They return around 11pm, very drunk. One of the younger ones stands naked on the pontoon while the oldest one turns the hose on him and the pile of clothing beside him. Then, for several hours, they set about what can only have been a competition among themselves to see who can make the most noise.

It is odd to hear French words shouted to the tune of *Roll out the Barrel*. They also howl, whistle, turn on some very loud music and appear to be taking hammers to the interior of the boat. It seems a joyless enterprise. There is no laughter, just maximum noise. By 1am every house along the waterfront has its bedroom lights on.

Early next morning a gloomy-looking Frenchman leaves the pontoon in search of breakfast. He passes a slender, white-haired local man fishing with a rod and line from the quay just beyond our stern. The elderly angler wears a neat, three-piece brown suit and a check deerstalker hat and nods a greeting to the yachtsman as he passes. The Frenchman ignores him.

The elderly and middle-aged of this town dress very stylishly and are very gracious. The streets are also very clean. It may be the absence of take-away food outlets, or the availability of dumpsters, although if you are abroad early you will see the shopkeepers at work with their brooms doing their stretch of the street; not just the sidewalk outside their premises but also the gutters and the street itself.

The other four Frenchmen emerge later, to urinate over the side of their boat and pace the pontoon with mobile telephones pressed to their ears. I am pegging out laundry by then but do not bother to acknowledge them. When you have observed people's penises hanging over their side rails, the usual civilities seem misplaced somehow. They leave at noon, and you wonder what it is in their affluent middle-class lives—or missing from it—that prompts them to behave like this, and whether they do it at home too or only abroad.

NEXT AFTERNOON JOSS AND The Girls line the outer pontoon, hands shading their eyes, looking down the harbor. A Rally is due, Joss says, and they have come to meet it. They wait and they wait and go away and come back and wait some more. Finally, early evening, half a dozen very expensive English motor yachts arrive. In my ignorance, the only rally I know of is the ARC, the annual Atlantic Rally for Cruisers where yachts-men sail across the Atlantic from the Canary Islands to the Caribbean and usually arrive tired and disheveled after several weeks at sea. These sailors have motored from Mallorca a few hours away and arrive immaculate in blazers and designer knitwear.

Joss and The Girls take their lines and secure the boats. Somewhere on board a button is pressed and a gangplank whirs down onto the pontoon. Another press of a button and handrails shoot up from it and snap into place. Then, while the rally members step ashore for cocktails, The Girls get to work. Elbows a blur, within the hour they have these boats hosed, buffed and flossed. They have barely evaporated from the pontoon before the rally members return to bathe and change for dinner at one of the restaurants down the quay.

In the early hours I wake to the sound of their voices coming back up. If you have ever envied people who live on pretty waterfronts or in picture postcard villages, all this nocturnal activity by summer visitors is food for thought if you like an undisturbed night's sleep. They are walking slowly and talking loudly, as people holidaying often do at night, as though everyone else in the world is on holiday too, and I wait patiently for them to troop past the houses and Voyager, through the gate and down the pontoon onto their boats. With them on the outer pontoon, and us tied to the quay, we are as far away from each other as it is possible to get, so once they are on board they can chat to their hearts' content and I, and the families in the five stuccoed houses, can go back to sleep. Unfortunately, two of the women settle themselves on the bench on the quay right alongside our boat, and four feet from the foot of our bed one of them proceeds to pour the miseries of her soul into the sympathetic ear of the other for the rest of the night.

I grope about, trying to find my earplugs without waking David. It is always a mystery to me how he can sleep through the most intrusive of human voices or late-night musicians, but the moment I even attempt to get out of bed he wakes with a start. Unable to find my earplugs I lie there, hearing her plaint and thinking about the nature of happiness and how affluence carries no guarantees. Sleep does finally arrive, however, just ahead of the truck coming to empty the dumpster on the quay.

EARLY NEXT MORNING a tall, spare man in his 50s, dressed in khaki shorts and shirt, taps on our hull to say he has berthed in front of us and will it inconvenience us. We peer round the side flaps of our awning and see that single-handedly he has shoehorned a large catamaran into the small space in front of us, a maneuver we had not seen, heard nor, more importantly, felt. David says, no problem, we aren't going anywhere, and the man disappears.

Sometime later, a young man recognizing the boat in front of us asks if the owner is about, saying that the last time he saw him was in Venezuela. Told no, he says, 'He'll be in a bar, then,' and looks behind him along the quay. David points out the nearest bar. 'No, too posh,' says the young man and goes in search of a more down-market one. By the time we rise, at seven next morning, he and his catamaran have gone, as quietly and unobtrusively as they arrived. A shy, courteous man. An Australian.

The weather is unstable. *El Niño* is blamed, a warming in the tropical Pacific which occurs every few years and affects weather patterns world-wide. Its name, *The Child*, refers to Christ, because of its original occurrence at Christmas time. In between the warm, pleasant, early summer days there are unseasonably hot windy ones, torrential rain, and one day there is a hailstorm, unheard of at this time of year. One morning we get up to find a fine reddish-brown coating over Voyager. All the boats are covered in it. So are all the parked cars, including the upholstery and interiors of quite a few whose windows and sun roofs have been left open overnight.

'What is it?' we ask Joss when he comes up the quay to check on one of the boats.

'Saharan dust,' he says.

Confronted with winds strong enough to lift and carry so much so far, you suddenly get a new perspective on biblical stories about plagues of frogs falling from the sky.

Like the weather, communications are also a little haphazard. So much European Union election material has been posted—postage-free for all the relevant political parties—that it sends the Spanish postal system into crisis. Even several weeks after voting has finished people are still complaining that it is taking a letter four weeks to get the few miles from Palma to Mahon. Our own priority, however, is to get some necessary work done on Voyager.

8

Mañana

....

Getting people to start work in Mahon has shades of *A Year in Provence* about it. Their arrival on the quay is usually to tell you that they have an urgent job on another boat leaving that afternoon so they won't be able to keep their appointment to work on Voyager. Their eyes, meanwhile, never quite meet yours.

'When, then?' you say.

'*Mañana*,' they say. 'For sure. Probably.'

It is only when they are safely trapped, bottom upwards, in one of your lockers, with an open tool box on the deck above them that you can feel relatively optimistic.

To be fair, the sailing season has started and everyone wants their boat prepared *now*. Although at the end of last season, in November, we did try to get a quote from a stainless-steel welder so that the work could be done during the winter. Despite reminders, by mid-May he still has not obliged, but we decide not to pursue it further on the principle that if it takes this long to get a quote, we shall be too old to sail by the time he gets around to the actual welding. Engagingly, nobody grumbles more than the Spanish themselves about the difficulty of getting anything done on time, or even at all. Then they shrug, spread their hands wide and say philosophically, 'This is Spain'.

Nevertheless, the electrician ultimately does the business with our automatic steering and work begins on resealing the windows. This involves removing each window, replacing the sealant between the glass and its aluminum frame, and then resealing the frame back into place. The window man is a Scandinavian called Sven who is not given to optimism. 'Maybe,' is as enthusiastic as he gets when asked if it will cure the leaking windows. The biggest problem is getting him to turn up. The second biggest is getting him to start work when he does.

'It's going to rain,' he'll say, squinting into a blistering blue cloudless sky. 'Can't risk taking one out today'.

Or, having done one window during the morning, he will return from lunch to say, 'Too late to start another one now. Tomorrow.'

Never do today what you can put off until *mañana*. This is Spain. It is part of its charm. You don't feel pressured because nobody puts any on you. 'Sure, you can leave it there … No hurry … No problem … Settle up tomorrow … This is Spain.'

None of this is to say that people do not work hard. They do. And none harder than the women who clean boats for Joss. In their 20s and 30s they arrive at the pontoon early morning, in bikinis and Marigold gloves, and without coffee or ciggie breaks or skiving off to the café on the quay they clean boats all day—and I mean *clean*—from power washers on the decks right down to old toothbrushes applied to the crevasses of teak stairs and the flossing of stainless steel bottle screws until they gleam.

We only see them pause once, to consider the name on an English boat they are working on. They look at us quizzically as we pass, on our way into town, in the hope of a translation. David and I glance at each other. Its equivalent in Spanish is unknown to us, and there is no mime we can think of that would not be a breach of public decency, so we shrug apologetically and walk on. Why anyone would want to call a boat Rumpy Pumpy is beyond me.

The evenings are glorious, sitting out in swimsuits, insect-free, the town and quay lit up and reflected in the water. And Venus rising.

9

Lift-Out

A t the beginning of June Voyager is lifted out for overdue bottom-scraping and anti-fouling at the boatyard down the end of the harbor. Naturally, with any kind of maneuver imminent, the wind will rise anyway, but today's forecast is for Force 6 or more. Given the inevitable delay to be expected—'This is Spain'—we have a plan in place for milling around indefinitely in what is a particularly cluttered part of the harbor in winds of 30 mph and rising but, unnervingly, the lifting team arrives at the ramp at the same moment we do, and the hoist is already in place.

In her time Voyager has been lifted out by hoist and by crane. Hoist is better. Not for her especially, but for me. Imagine your home swinging over your head on the end of a chain and you will know what I mean. And, just as the furniture removers always walk into your house and say the estimator hasn't ordered a big enough van, so the crane driver always starts muttering at the last minute that they haven't sent a big enough crane and you start to panic about it toppling over with your boat on it. Even with a hoist, however, they do not disappoint. On the dock the man in charge of it eyes Voyager and purses his lips.

'You five meters wide?' he asks.

'Yes,' says David.

'Might just make it then.'

The hoist driver is tall, fair, speaks clipped but excellent English and everything runs like a precision watch; including the Force 6 which does not arrive until after we are safely settled on the hard, when it roars through the boatyard sweeping before it wood shavings, paint trays and rollers, several small children and a stray dog. It leaves behind it a coating of dust and grit, to the especial chagrin of the matronly lady next door who had spent the entire morning varnishing the extensive woodwork on her immaculate motor yacht, and who will now have to rub it all down again. Further down the yard a voice pleads for someone to come and prop his ladder back up so that he can get down off his boat.

Meanwhile our hired power-washer arrives exactly on cue and, for the first and only time ever, anywhere, we are handed a scraper as well. This is Spain? Over the next three hours we power-wash and scrape her, removing enough marine life from her hulls to keep the Discovery Channel busy for a whole series. The window man arrives, says 'Tomorrow. If it doesn't rain,' and drives away again.

IT IS VERY HOT and humid. Even the Spanish are complaining about it. We start at six each morning, before it is light, to get as much done in the exposed places as possible before the sun rises. For the minute it does, it is like an oven. Early evening it is still in the 90s. The sunsets are buttercup gold.

Over the next week we undercoat and anti-foul Voyager, polish her topsides, service both engines and gearboxes, clean and paint the propellers, and David is finally able to complete the gelcoat repair on the port bow begun in Bayona last year. While waiting for the replacement sacrificial anodes that somebody in town forgot to order and which the supplier in Madrid air-freights only once a week—'on Wednesdays'—we also fit new hinges to the hatches so they stay open on their own like they used to, instead of having to be propped up with bits of stick. Gradually, by stealth, we even get some more of the windows done.

There is also David's heroic struggle with the two cables which connect the engines in the hulls to the stop mechanisms on the cockpit control panel. Each cable is around twenty feet long, wends a long and complicated route through the bowels of each hull, and both have seized almost solid. When the cockpit is filled with dismantled control panel, the entire contents of the big toolbox, lots of oily rag and David in elbow-wielding overdrive, it is usually prudent to find something to do below. At one stage he can be glimpsed through the companionway doors with twenty feet of cable coiling round him, and at another is to be heard muttering, 'Well, I've either fixed it, or cocked it up entirely.'

I HAD REACHED QUITE an advanced age before discovering that the planet had on it such a thing as a sacrificial anode. When I found out what replacing one entailed, I should have been quite happy never to have encountered one at all. Voyager's are 10-inch-long heavy blocks of zinc and they are there to stop the electrolyc action in seawater from eroding any metal components exposed to it. The zinc, being a soft metal, is eaten away—or sacrificed—leaving undamaged the harder metals of the propellers and rudders.

Naturally, these anodes must be replaced before the zinc is completely eroded or the electrolyc action will begin attacking the props and rudders. Ours are bolted through the hulls and require David outside on a ladder with a spanner tightening a nut, and me inside the engine bay with a spanner stopping the bolt head from turning. Failure to tighten the nut sufficiently could result in us sinking at sea.

To secure the bolt head on the inside I have to crouch in the engine bay where there is room for only one foot to stand flat. The other, braced against the curved inside of the hull, slides remorselessly down to meet its partner where, made silkily mobile by the merest trace of engine oil, they proceed to fold over each other until my shuffling resembles a Cossack dancer who has lost the plot. To overcome this, and get some purchase on my spanner, I really need to brace myself against something solid; but I can't, since any attempt to do so brings tender bits of flesh into contact with sharp bits of engine.

When the nut is properly tightened David comes in and hauls me out of the engine bay, fits poly bags onto my tainted feet for the hobble over the bridge deck to the other engine bay, and there we repeat the process all over again. This is the problem with catamarans—as owners of single-hulled boats are forever eager to remind you during haul-outs—you have to do everything twice.

WHEN YOU LIVE ON a boat you discover what floats about in the water which, once treated, you will ultimately drink. When your boat is made of white plastic you also discover what is floating about in the air you breathe. Local yachtsmen call the deposits from the power station at the end of the harbor *yellow rain*. It results in tiny yellow spots which will neither wash nor scrub off your gelcoat, but have to be polished off with cutting compound.

I am standing on our side deck removing yellow rain from the coach house roof when the hoist travels alongside, very precisely, barely a couple of feet away, with a 55-footer in its slings ready to go back into the water. The driver is standing, as always very tall and fair and straight, at his controls on the side of his hoist. As he passes me, eyeball to eyeball, he says, 'Gut morning,' very formally in his clipped, precise English, and such is the impression of two passing U-boat captains on their conning towers, that I barely stop myself from saluting.

10

Life Ashore

We have the yard pretty much to ourselves. Like all boatyards, part of it is a graveyard of dreams: restoration projects which people have started but then become overwhelmed by the amount of work required; long-term ventures like our own which have run aground; or the perfect idea for carefree family weekends and holidays afloat, only the wife and kids hated it.

On the other boats around us, people mostly come for a few hours in the evenings and at the weekend. Since we spend a lot of time up-ended in lockers, inside the hulls or in between them, we get to recognize our neighbors as much by sound as sight. Mozart's Requiem means the man with the wooden ketch has come to spend a few hours on it after work. Heavy metal means he has paid his son to do a few hours of paint-stripping for him. Prolonged rasping means La Señora on the motor yacht is sandpapering her woodwork again, prior to yet another coat of varnish. Metallic clangs interspersed with the occasional dull thud mean the power boat owner has brought his two bored adolescent sons with him and they are using a paint tin lid as a Frisbee, to the detriment of everybody's gelcoat but their own.

Gradually these other boat owners stop by. La Señora's husband offers the use of his car to fetch bread and milk. The Mozart-lover tells us where he lives and says if we visit that bay anytime to call in for a cup of tea with him and his family. His son takes the opportunity to hone his English as he enquires about our progress.

They're keen, the Spanish, on polishing their English. I cannoned into a young man in town one day, and when you're startled you forget all your carefully-rehearsed foreign phrases and revert to your own language. 'Oh!' I said, taking his elbow briefly to steady him, 'I'm *so* sorry.' When I joined David, a few yards away, he was looking past me and smiling. I turned and looked back. The young Spaniard was still where I had left him but mouthing something to himself slowly with great concentration while rhythmically stretching out his hand.

'What's he doing?' I whispered.

'Practicing an English apology,' said David.

Early evenings the security men do a tour of inspection and lock the gates. Arc lights worthy of a football stadium provide virtual daylight in the cockpit to dine by, and we are kings of the castle, high up on a high boat with an uninterrupted view across the harbor to the twinkling lights of the town. There is also a demented bird. Deceived by the arc lights, it thinks it is still day. It is tired but it keeps on tweeting.

One evening, after the gates are locked, three shouting men on a cart race a thin brown horse with all its ribs showing down the hard, shiny, sloping road. The horse's head is thrown back and its eyes are wild. Its back legs collapse under it and the men shout louder than ever. It struggles up, desperate to pacify them, and they race it on down the road. A dog barks, locked inside a container yard below the boatyard.

WE ARE MILES FROM any shops here and David cycles up an enormous hill, in the horrendous heat, for the things we need. It would kill me, but he does it cheerfully, and along with undercoat and pop rivets will return with bags of plump red cherries and the delectable crème caramel pastries they sell in the little square above the fish market.

Meanwhile I sit under the boat in the shade, and contemplate the nature of happiness. I am sanding the hull below the waterline and scraping barnacles away from nooks and crannies that are hard to reach. One neighbor's radio is blaring tuneless pop music; another's anti-fouling paint stinks to high heaven; the wind is blowing dust all over me; I am crouched on a lump of wood with an old cushion on it to keep its splinters from piercing my shorts, and I ease the cramp in my right hand by alternating between a rusty craft knife and a scrap of frayed sandpaper wrapped around a wood off-cut found in the boatyard's dumpster—and I am ridiculously happy.

IT IS STARTLING, THOUGH, how quickly one's living conditions descend into squalor when a facility taken for granted, such as the instantaneous and hygienic disposal of waste water, disappears. Each application of undercoat and antifouling paint on the hulls needs to be thoroughly dry before we let water out of the sinks, which would simply wash streaks of the new paint off again. This means pouring every drop of water that you normally put down a plughole—for personal washing, teeth brushing, greasy washing up, water strained from boiled vegetables and all those other liquid dribs and dregs—into a slop bucket to be carried from the galley into the cockpit, over the stern, down a ladder and across the yard for disposal.

On the way back you carry half the boatyard's grit back up onto your deck on the bottom of your shoes, where it mixes with windborne dirt, sawdust, fiberglass grindings and heavy dew, which you can not wash off because it will run down the hulls with their still-moist undercoat or hugely expensive anti-fouling paint.

Nor is the dirt confined to the decks and cockpit. With windows being taken out, the dust feels free to move indoors. And despite removing our shoes at the stern the minute we step off the ladder, the crustaceans we scraped from our hulls are now mysteriously embedded in the carpets.

In just four days, in fact, life has become primitive. It is also tiring. But at least we have the water we need on tap. As I walk my slop bucket daily I reflect on how even more tiring it must be for those millions who have to walk miles daily to fetch their water in the first place. On the way to dispose of our dirty water I also dispose of our daily poly bag of domestic rubbish and contemplate the amount of non-biodegradable waste we advanced nations inflict upon the planet daily.

As I lie in bed awaiting sleep before another pre-dawn start, eyes screwed up tight against the glare of the boatyard's arc lights through uncurtained windows, I ponder once more that great existential question: how *does* a mosquito know when you're dropping off? You can keep very still for ages, ready to swat it, and it simply lies doggo somewhere out of sight but the moment blessed sleep begins to wash over you ... nyahhhh, right against your ear.

AT LAST WE ARE able to jettison the slop bucket and turn on the hose. When a large ladybug lands on our immaculate cockpit sole I ask it if its feet are clean. It seems unable to take off again from the wet surface and sooner or later one of us will forget it is there and tread on it. So I lift it onto the life raft, where it stands for a while, opening and closing its delicate red and white spotted casing and exposing transparent and surprisingly-creased wings before shuffling its waterlogged feet and flying away. Watching it, you wonder how anything so small and fragile manages to survive on a planet that has us crashing about on it.

La Señora's woodwork, glowing in the late evening sun, is a lovely sight, although I might have been tempted to use a matt varnish on the steps and hand rails. One careless move on that high-gloss finish could send you spinning overboard. David winces and says he would hate to be the bloke who tries to put it back in the water without marking anything.

'Bet they're all planning to be ill that day,' he says.

With all the scraping and polishing, my right arm, shoulder and neck feel as if they have been off on their own somewhere and then come back to recuperate after being involved in some terrible accident. However, everything that needs to be done while Voyager is out of the water has now been done and Sven can finish resealing the windows back on the pontoon. We arrange to go back in the water next morning.

'Force 7,' says Sven gloomily when we tell him. 'Next three days. And it'll get worse.'

We enjoy a perfect re-launch, probably the most stress-free ever, and sail back down the harbor to our old berth. The arrival of a near-gale-force wind does, for once, actually justify Sven's Jonah-like prediction, but not until we are safely tied up.

Sunset is at five minutes past nine tonight. At the naval base opposite they play the national anthem and someone makes a brief speech before *Taps*. I wake at 1am. Despite my locking the gate before going to bed dozens of youths are running up and down the pontoon although, with typical Spanish politeness, they do not board any of the boats. The quay beyond is full of them. Hundreds of them.

David stirs. 'Wassamatter?'

'Must be a fiesta or something.'

'Um?'

'It can't be up to much if they're running about down here on a deserted pontoon.'

'Um.' He turns over and goes back to sleep.

The terrible injuries the upper right side of my body sustained while

AWOL are throbbing piteously. I fall back on my pillow convinced I shall not close my eyes again this night, but within minutes I am comatose, apparently; at least I am aware of nothing more until daylight streams in through the hatch above my head and there is the sound of knocking on our hull. On the one occasion I could really have done without him, Sven has come early to reseal the last of the windows.

11

Cala Grao

We leave Mahon in mid-June. The plan is to visit a few bays around Menorca; partly for pure enjoyment, but also to ensure that everything on board works properly before undertaking any long hauls. Our plan for the summer is to head for Sardinia and then round Sicily to the Greek islands before returning to Gibraltar prior to heading out into the Atlantic. As if to confirm the wisdom of our trip around the bays, the GPS on its first outing in seven months says the distance to our first destination, Cala Grao, is 515 miles, but finally settles on the actual six.

Cala Grao is a quiet bay with a small fishing village of white-walled houses and red bougainvillea. In a beautiful, tranquil evening, pink and shiny from the sunset, we paddle over to the waterside Bar de Moll for a beer. On the edge of the little quay half a dozen mallard ducks stand in a line, their jeweled green heads bobbing up and down like piano hammers, determined not to be moved from their chosen spot as they enjoy the last of the day's sunshine. Ultimately the dinghy gets too close for comfort, their nerve cracks, and they throw themselves into the water protesting noisily and paddling away single file, indignant at losing face.

The only other customers are two English couples. The two women turn out to be former nurses at our local hospital at home. When we return to the boat, the people now anchored in front of us are from the area in Wales where we sailed Voyager before setting out. It suddenly seems to be quite a small world.

AROUND 6.30 NEXT MORNING a fisherman ties a small open boat to the quay. He fetches an icebox from his lock-up and sets about sorting and

42

cleaning the best of his catch. The cleaned fish he throws into the icebox, the rest he tosses to the patiently waiting seagulls.

After our own breakfast we set off for the lagoon to visit the famous Albufera des Gran nature reserve. You used to be able to dinghy right into its lagoon from the harbor but the stream that provided access silted up during last autumn's storms, so we have to walk across the beach. It is filled with hundreds of school children, brought here by coaches. The noise is horrendous, but as you continue walking the sound diminishes from a howl to a hum and by the time you reach the lagoon there is only the hum of an insect. We see a small lizard, a dozen seagulls and a couple of wading birds, but otherwise the reserve's wildlife eludes us. It is a magical walk through the woods, however, among wild olive trees, tree spurge and Aleppo pines.

One of the advantages of our way of traveling is that some of the quietest beaches are accessible only, or most easily, by boat. In the afternoon we take the dinghy down a shallow channel to Isla Longa for a swim. We have the beach to ourselves. Behind it there is a large deserted house, white with green shutters. It has a large well for domestic water and a series of terraced gardens sheltered by rows of mature pines. It is cool and shady and looks a lovely place to live. You wonder why no-one lives in such a house, who used to, and why they don't any more.

12

Addaya

Next morning we leave for another bay. Cala de Addaya. It gets windy and almost on the nose which makes for an uncomfortable trip with waves hitting the starboard bow. The foredeck is soon awash but we are happy to see that despite this none of the windows leak.

Addaya is a long, narrow, beautifully-protected bay, the far end of which the chart shows to be very shallow. The top end is crowded with anchored boats that have a much deeper draught than ours, so we carry on down, over a sand bar leaving only eighteen inches of clear water beneath us, and anchor towards the end of the bay in five feet. Voyager draws only three and a quarter feet and, with two hulls, even if we do touch bottom it just means the crockery rattles a bit and we have to go into reverse a bit sharpish. She won't fall over on her side like a monohull with a deep keel tends to do. Once settled down the end of the bay, we put up the awning and mix some Sangria.

This *cala* resembles a Scottish loch, apart from the cicadas. Apparently, during the last British incursion of Menorca, in 1798, the Navy couldn't get its ships into Cala de Fornells because of bad weather and came here instead. The men of a Scottish battalion, waking to its low hills and heather, thought they were home again. As if to reinforce the comparison for us, our Navtex provides a gale warning for the Scottish Hebrides.

The bay is bliss. So are the glorious sunny days and the starry nights with their bright slender moon. We potter around the bay in the dinghy and take the odd trip into the village for fresh bread and fruit, then back to sangria and shady seclusion. The only other person we see for several

44

days is a tall, spare, stooped man in dark shorts and singlet who wades out to some distinctive rocks quite some distance below us early one morning and seems to be inspecting seaweed.

And it is so quiet you could hear a pin drop; except for one morning when we are shot awake at dawn by an exploding duck under the bed. At least, that is what it sounds like. Raucous at the best of times, the demands of a hungry young duck are magnified many times in the natural echo chamber created by a catamaran's two hulls. When I stick my head out of the hatch there are eight of them milling about waiting for breakfast. Once fed, they bob away towards the village, in a tight little group, looking particularly vulnerable and small. In the late afternoons the cicadas rest and the woodpigeons take over. Between 6pm and 8pm a donkey brays.

At the weekend an occasional small boat ventures down. A traditional sailing dinghy with a family of four in it, tacks a little too close to the wind to get around us. The man's face passes level with our stern, grimacing at his efforts and waggling a hand in embarrassment. He soon gets it together, however, and fairly hurtles back up to the village. A motor launch—an open boat generally used for river trips, of varnished wood and immaculate seating—takes a stately poodle down, but before I can tidy up in case its captain pops over with a visiting card it poodles away again. A young couple in a small open power boat, with the name of a water sports company on its side, anchor as far down the bay and as far from us as they can get. Then they become invisible for five hours. At dusk the boat chugs past with the man looking smug and the girl glancing a little furtively at our boat. We are below, so it is we who are invisible now, and she looks relieved at not seeing anyone.

The evenings are glorious with every tint and hue of crimson, scarlet and gold. I have foresworn any more photographs of sunsets, though. You are surrounded by this mesmerizing explosion of color, of refracted light and shimmering water; an elemental assault on the senses making you one with all nature—with the universe, even. Then you get your prints back from the developer and there's this reddish blob with a needle-thin reflection on rather murky-looking water.

WE ARE STILL STRUGGLING to get regular weather forecasts. Monaco Radio puts one out first in French and then in English. Unfortunately, sometimes they forget to do the English version. When they remember, being on short wave and from such a distance, it is often barely audible. Even when we can hear it, it is sometimes confusing. For instance, when a British shipping forecast says, 'gale later' you know that means later in the second half of the 24-hour period covered by this particular forecast. The French will say, 'gale next night,' and you sit there mulling over whether they mean, 'tonight', '*later* tonight' or maybe even 'tomorrow night'.

Our radio is not only capable of tuning into short wave transmissions, such as Monaco Radio, but can also pick up single side band (SSB) transmissions. SSB is a ham radio frequency for mariners and some people transmit forecasts which they have received from other sources. David tunes in and picks up the UK Maritime Net which is a group of British cruisers in the Mediterranean who chat to one another at a regular time on a designated channel and often put out a weather forecast, although not consistently or at a specific time. So you have to listen to the whole broadcast.

Unfortunately, the channel used by the Maritime Net is subject to a very determined saboteur who whistles, howls and plays music, so that the Net's broadcast becomes incomprehensible. When the Net changes channels, so does the saboteur. On one day the only forecast available is for Portugal because that is the only request the Net has received, but today, finally, we do get a forecast for where we are. There is a weather front crossing the Mediterranean, bringing winds of up to 46mph, or Gale Force 8.

We had been planning to move on to Fornells, that superbly-protected bay which the Scottish battalion had been unable to enter because of bad weather and had sequestered here among the heather at Addaya instead. We decide to remain here also, for the couple of days it will take the front to pass over. We do a few chores while we wait and I volunteer to clean the salt and dirt off our radar dome, half way up the mast, to improve the quality of the signal. I prepare a sponge with soapy water and climb aloft with it in a poly bag attached to my belt.

Heights send me peculiar, so I get up to the dome by not looking down, but once there my arm muscles are too puny to support my body weight with one hand long enough to sponge the dome with the other. Then my supporting hand begins to sweat with the effort and very soon holding on even with both hands becomes a problem. So I come down and David goes up and washes the radar dome, only I've added too much washing-up liquid to the sponge and the equipment is deluged in soap suds and so is he.

TONIGHT CLOUD HIDES THE moon and stars. The wind gets up, as the forecast promised, and we take in the awning to stop it flapping through the night. But we still find it too rough to sleep after the former tranquility of our private lake and get up for a game of cards. As the wind increases one of the genoa shackles in the cockpit begins to rattle frenetically and David goes out to silence it.

'I think we may be dragging,' he calls down to me.

I join him in the cockpit. It is difficult to see immediately, going into a dark night from a lighted saloon.

'We weren't so close to this outcrop, were we?' he asks pointing.

Each person's eyes adjust differently. Some people can take half an hour to get their night vision and then lose it in seconds. Some adjust fast and keep it regardless, even with torches being flashed in their faces. My sense of distance may be rubbish, but my night vision is fast. I can see that the outcrop David is pointing at is not the one opposite which we have been anchored for some days, but a similar one further down the bay.

I can also see that directly beyond our stern and only a short way away are those once-distant jagged rocks where the tall, spare man in the dark shorts and singlet appeared to be inspecting seaweed. The wind, currently roaring straight down through the bay's entrance, is driving us towards them.

Suddenly it is headless chicken time as we run down into the hulls, switch on the engine batteries, rush back up, start the engines, and raise our anchor with its half ton of mud and weed which has to be scraped off before we can attempt to put it down again. We try several times to re-anchor, even using two anchors, but both drag. So much mud and weed comes up on the second anchor that David is unable to lift it back on deck again. We decide to go up and join all the other boats where we assume the holding must be better.

I find it a struggle to steer up the narrow stretch of bay in pitch darkness into a 35mph wind. A rocky outcrop looms suddenly out of the blackness. I over-steer and accelerate to avoid it and end up heading for another on the opposite side. With such an erratic, zigzag course it is a miracle I don't hurl David overboard, hanging as he is, head-first over the bow trying to prise glutinous mud off the anchors.

To unsettle the nerves even more, the windmill of our wind generator begins howling like a banshee. We will discover subsequently that in winds up to Force 6, and from Gale Force 8 and above, it behaves perfectly normally, but in a Force 7 it goes into overdrive and screams like something from the nether regions. There is no way to stop it now though, not without losing fingers, even if we were able to leave what we are doing to go and restrain it.

When we finally reach the top of the narrow channel and approach the wider, deeper section of water of the main anchorage we are confronted by a Maltese boat. It is directly ahead of us and charging back and forth. It is one of those boats, familiar in any anchorage, that constantly shunts, even in the lightest airs: up over its anchor, yank; back out on the full extent of its chain, yank; up over the anchor again, yank; endlessly. In the present conditions it has become hyper-active. We judge our time carefully to avoid a collision and make our way round it into the anchorage.

It is bedlam. Most of the boats are dragging. Those few still attached to the bottom are swinging violently, but each one is out of sync with its neighbor so that they are effectively charging at one another. Some people are letting out more chain and compounding the problem; others flash torches and shout at each other in French, English, Swedish and Spanish. And all around us the night roars, everybody's wind generator whines and ours screams.

We motor around in the noise and flashing lights looking for a space to anchor. We find somewhere, not quite large enough but it will do if the anchor bites immediately. It doesn't. We try again and fail again but this time a wind gust drives us rapidly towards rocks. We motor away quickly and search for another spot, but without success and decide finally that our only option is to go back and try the area behind the Maltese boat.

We drag once more, rushing backwards into the narrow, rock-strewn channel. We are about to haul the anchor up again when Voyager comes suddenly to a halt with her stern in the channel a few yards from rocks. We hold our breath and wait. After a few minutes of staring at the rocks in the darkness, we feel confident enough to leave off watching and address the screaming banshee on our afterdeck. David snares it with the boathook and I tie a rope around it.

The improvement in your mental state when intolerable noise suddenly stops is enormous. I make us a hot drink and we sit and discuss what we should do. We have two problems. The first is that if we drag again we should have very little time to respond. The second is that if the wind changes direction we will swing into jagged rocks on the other side of the channel.

We decide to stay where we are. Although it is not a good place to be, at least the anchor is holding. And we are away from other boats. But we must be vigilant. We keep a watch together for a while, in case the anchor goes suddenly and one of us needs to man the controls while the other raises the anchor. But as time passes, thanks to the strength of the wind, the anchor seems to be digging in pretty well. Meanwhile, the other boats drag and drift for hours. In particular, a large English motor yacht takes forever to re-anchor. It is one of those traditional wooden boats, highly varnished with brass fittings, that are sometimes referred to as 'a gentleman's motor yacht'.

IT IS ALWAYS FASCINATING what a difference a few hours make afloat. After a chaotic night of frenzied activity, by the following afternoon the anchorage has a touch of a 1930s English tea room about it. Some boats have left during the morning and some, like us, have re-anchored. Alongside us now is the gentleman's motor yacht that had so much difficulty re-anchoring during the night. It has brass paraffin lamps in the wheelhouse and two sit-up-and-beg bicycles on the stern. Its Skipper and the Memsahib wear wide-brimmed Tilley hats with chinstraps and have the couple from a similar yacht, which has only recently arrived, over for afternoon tea. They sit on the afterdeck around a tea table laid with a white cloth and bone china cups and saucers and haw-haw and boom like Bertie Wooster and his chums.

13

Fornells

....

Wﾠe are now into a period of more stable weather and I take the helm as we make the nine mile passage from Addaya to Fornells. We have not yet had the sails out this year and decide to have a look at them. They are a bit dirty from the Saharan dust at Mahon but, with the wind averaging only 3mph, having aired them we put them away again.

Menorca contains an extraordinary concentration of prehistoric remains. As well as Neolithic villages and caves the island is littered with Bronze Age burial mounds, funeral chambers in the form of an upturned boat, and T-shaped monuments which were probably altars. You pass them at the side of a road or climbing a grassy hill, unfenced and unheralded, a reminder of continuity and time passing. Most beguiling of them all are the large stone burial mounds which overlook the sea. They are thought to have covered a family funerary chamber, with a wooden house built on top. And as you sail around the island, gazing up at the cliffs, one of them will appear above you and, suddenly, there is Bronze Age man staring back down at you.

As you think of the people who have lived and died here over the centuries you wonder, despite some theories, if the original inhabitants of islands like these really did die out; or whether their genes are still alive and well and tending their crops behind the dry stone walls of the market gardens, or weighing your fruit and vegetables in the local market. Some years ago, after the development of DNA for forensic purposes, researchers took samples from the residents of a southern English village and compared them with some taken from human remains excavated from a nearby prehistoric burial mound. They discovered that many of the people in the village were descendents of the man in the ancient tomb.

Perhaps even more extraordinary is the recollection of Laurie Lee, author of *Cider with Rosie*, in a radio interview many years ago, concerning another ancient mound in his native Cotswolds. As each new generation came to consciousness, the parents in the villages within sight of the mound would answer their children's inevitable question by telling them, 'It's where the little prince is buried'. When 20th century archaeologists finally burrowed into the mound they identified it as the final resting place of a Bronze Age chieftain. What so captured Laurie Lee's imagination was the fact that knowledge of the mound's purpose and incumbent had been passed, unbroken, by word of mouth for something like 150 generations, from the Bronze Age to the present day.

As a famous archaeologist once observed, everything is always older than you think.

CALA DE FORNELLS IS a large shallow bay some two miles long and three-quarters of a mile wide. It has a small whitewashed, palm-fringed village, also called Fornells, on its western shore, and two small islands lying off its eastern edge. The bay's narrow entrance provides excellent protection and it attracts leisure boats of all kinds. Down at its far end, there is a little hamlet called Salinas Vellas. The water there is an ideal depth for anchoring boats like ours. To reach it we have to pass the super yachts, which need the deeper water. One has seven deck levels, plus integral helicopter and enough communications technology festooning its bridge to control a space mission.

The bay is home to very small boats, too. Those belonging to the local fishermen bob on buoys in the shallows while the dinghies from the sailing school—especially the single-handed Piccolos with their vivid mauve sails—quiver like flocks of exotic butterflies.

David rigs our own dinghy into sailing mode and on windy days we go out with the boy racers, the Hobie cats, and the wind surfers, flying along at speeds impossible with our small outboard. It is exhilarating. The lack of an outboard, however, does create a problem in getting back on board a boat swinging at anchor. In high winds the answer is a full-out run down Voyager's side, a flying right-hand turn and a feverish grab at her stern.

By contrast, in light airs we bob along with the beginners and the unhurried little tour boat called *La Pinta* and after a blissful dawdle around the bay return home horizontal with our feet dangling over the dinghy's sides.

During the hottest part of the day we simply sit in the shade of our awning and the bay's denizens come to us. Three Spaniards on a Laser—one hanging from its trapeze with a terrified face—roar contradictory instructions at one another as they hurtle past. An apprentice windsurfer, his concentration and back muscles devoted to staying upright, is eager to show off his newly-acquired skills. He is using our starboard quarter as a marker. As he hurtles towards it, his eyes widen with the recognition that he has miscalculated. There is a howl as he falls off his board, a better alternative than impaling himself on one of our davits. A canoe passes with two panama-hatted women in it, straight-backed, paddles synchronized. In between them sits a huge black dog, as tall and straight-backed as they are, but motionless apart from its great head turning slowly and rhythmically from side to side as it observes the scenery. Small children on the nearby diving pontoon cry '*Olá!*' in high, fluting voices as they hurl themselves into the water. A naked middle-aged woman throws herself repeatedly off the stern of the German boat next door.

Most places have something memorable about them: sounds, smells, sights or tastes. Fornells has a peacock. It calls in the early evening and a horse whinnies in reply. Someone in the little hamlet of Salinas Vellas is learning to play the trumpet. At first the notes seem as mournful and tuneless as the peacock's, but over a period of days the strains of *I Did It My Way* become recognizable.

Fornells' restaurants are famous for their lobster stew, but a bowl each costs more than our weekly food bill so we leave it for the super yachts and patronize the local baker instead. His shop is in the small village square and his pies and pastries come hot from the oven. We chug carefully back in the dinghy with a warm tuna pie dangling in a bag from one hand, a ham and cheese lattice on the other, and a chocolate confection balanced across the knees. Healthy living? Forget it! Being rather partial to a really good savory pie, after tasting these we return again and again.

14

Cuitadella

W e take a taxi from the quay early one morning and spend the day in Cuitadella. The cruising guide emphasizes how crowded its narrow harbor is in high summer and we are concerned about the difficulties of finding a space wide enough to berth a catamaran. A taxi ride makes a nice change and gives us a chance to see more of the island's interior. Menorca is famous for its cheeses and much of the land is given over to dairy farming, dotted here and there with a few small villages and the occasional market town. The taxi is air-conditioned and so bitingly cold that it is a relief to emerge into the warmth of Cuitadella.

The name means *little city* in Aragonese and it was once the island's capital. The Romans used it, and the Moors. When the Aragonese expelled the Moors they also rebuilt the town. Corsairs then attacked it repeatedly until finally it was razed by the Turkish pirate, Barbarrossa—Red Beard—in 1558, who also carried off many of the inhabitants to Istanbul's slave market. The survivors re-built the town behind fortified walls, in the grand style with grand mansions, some with colonnaded loggias along their frontages where today you can buy a sarong or sit and have a cup of coffee. Tiny artisans' houses in blind alleys also survive; built that way, it is said, to discourage invaders by making them fearful of becoming trapped.

It is a lovely old town whose architecture was saved as a result of a military decision. In 1722 the British, the occupying force at the time, transferred the capital to Mahon because of its superior harbor. So while Mahon developed, Cuitadella and its old nobility stagnated. In doing so, however, it escaped further foreign architectural influences and its beautiful old centre has been preserved intact. It sits high above the harbor and with its street markets of local goods is a very pleasant place to wander.

The harbor itself has been in use for more than three and a half thousand years, since long before even the Phoenicians arrived. As well as being long and narrow it is also difficult to enter under certain weather conditions. And although sheltered, it is subject to sea swell at times, which gets an added boost from the wash caused by commercial vessels, including the regular ferry service. It is nevertheless very popular with yachtsmen and is very crowded. And we are glad we came by taxi today.

Like the town above it, however, it is very picturesque. We stroll along much of its length and enjoy a three-course lunch at one of the restaurants on its quay. Quite early on in the meal David falls victim to an exploding mussel. He rarely leaves a tablecloth unmarked by his presence, but always claims it is not his fault. The mussel, he says, shot from his fingers, spiraled upward and landed on the cloth. I missed this, having been distracted by the large, temperature-controlled lobster tank at the restaurant next door. One of its temporary residents is gazing at me with mute but eloquent pleading.

'How could you eat it once you'd looked it in the eyes?' I say to our waiter. 'It's just too personal.' He nods compassionately. His restaurant doesn't have a lobster tank.

Thankfully, our taxi ride back to Fornells is less chilly than the journey here.

15

Fornells to Mahon

Next morning I wake at 6am into a day too beautiful to stay in bed any longer. Beyond our stern is a very small hill with a rectangular stone house on it. A full moon—huge and russet gold—is slowly setting behind the stone house. It is an image from a cartoon: a circle behind a rectangle on a pyramid, in intense glowing color, unreal and unbelievably lovely.

Our awakening the following morning is anything but tranquil. At 4 o'clock we come roaring out of sleep and struggling to our feet simultaneously. There is a shrieking, the like of which we have never heard before. It pierces the brain and drives us up onto the bridge deck with two compulsions: to know what is causing it and to make it stop. Its cause becomes apparent as soon as we near the galley: it is the propane gas alarm.

Gas! We are leaking gas! A spark causes an explosion. A switch causes a spark. Don't switch any lights on!

And with images of airborne body parts filling our minds we blunder about in the dark, throwing open all the hatches in some muddled notion of reducing the impact of the inevitable explosion.

But since gas is heavier than air and finds its lowest level, it won't be up at hatch level, will it? It will be filling the bilges, won't it?

While I rush out into the cockpit to man the bilge pump, David tears up the galley floor coverings and the bilge-covers below the gas stove and water heater, which is where the gas alarm sensors are located. He comes to fetch me from my fevered pumping in the cockpit.

'You've got a stronger sense of smell than me,' he shouts above the screeching, and moments later his hands are round my ankles and I'm head-first into the bilge.

'Nothing,' I shout, the word echoing around me from the bilge's sides.

Although there is no smell of gas, and we have done everything we can to expel even the slightest traces of any that might exist, still the alarm tears into our brains. We cannot bear the unbearable sound any longer and David disconnects the wires of the alarm. After a few minutes respite from that terrible clamor, the brain can begin to function rationally again and David notices that the battery volt meter is showing a very low reading.

The gas detector has a safety circuit which sets off an alarm when it has insufficient power to perform its task. And that is what it has been doing; not telling us that there is gas about, but that it has too little power to detect any if there *should* be a leak. We turn off all the electrical circuits to relieve the batteries and go back to bed. Later that morning, after running an engine to recharge them we discover they are not holding a charge. When batteries go, they go quickly. We need new ones, but there is nowhere to buy the sort we need at Fornells. Our best option is to return to Mahon.

IT IS A FOUR-HOUR journey. When we are just over an hour away I swear I can smell crème caramel pastries. Our old spot on Joss's pontoon is unavailable because of a weekend regatta, but he lets us tie up to his crane dock further down the quay. With water on tap again we embark on two weeks' laundry and a general clean up.

We are not alone in tackling personal hygiene. Just yards from us an elderly man is encouraging an elderly Labrador off the quay and into the water. The dog is reluctant, but finally succumbs to its innate sense of loyalty. At first we fear the dog is being drowned. Then we realize he is being given a bath. The man and his dog live in a cave across the quay from our berth. The cave has a brown wooden door with a crop of healthy-looking string beans growing up canes on either side of it and a small patch of grass in front. He is not supposed to still live there, apparently, just use it as a chalet. But early next morning his presence is betrayed by two seagulls waiting at his door for their breakfast.

When next we see him, the elderly man is sitting on a short-legged chair on the quay cleaning a fish he has just caught. While he gets his dinner, as men there have done here since the Stone Age, on the other side of us another man earns his bread by using his tug with impressive skill to ease a tanker past us, stern-first out of its confined commercial berth and into open water. Suddenly, the steel hawser between them snaps. There is a great disappearing of heads from rails and quay as it flails wildly like an angry snake, but the tug boat skipper has it under control and another one attached within moments and all the heads pop up again, like prairie dogs.

As for ourselves, our laundry is done, our food cupboards are re-stocked and our new batteries are in place. We are ready to move on again. This time the plan is to leave the Spanish island of Menorca for the Italian island of Sardinia.

Sardinia

16

Menorca to Sardinia

Today is the first day of July. At 7 o'clock Voyager slips from the quay into a still morning. I take her out. As we motor down the harbor under a bright blue sky there is a full moon setting to starboard and a huge rising sun to port. The sea is so calm that even beyond the heads there are no waves, just an unbroken surface quivering—the way water does in the washing-up bowl when the engines are idling—as if the planet is vibrating ever so gently.

Three hours later the sea is very roly and we have porpoises alongside. An hour after that the sea has settled back into a gentle rhythm with just enough wind to put out the genoa. We also put up the cockpit awning, making it shady and restful. Just us, in a big, blue empty sea.

During the afternoon, over the course of several hours, a large number of turtles of varying sizes paddle laboriously towards us wearing that look of intense concentration peculiar to reptiles on the move. They are so close to us as they pass that they are almost touching our sides. It is unknown, in our experience, for a turtle to get so close. They usually dive and disappear long before a boat gets anywhere near them.

From the size of some of these, they must be quite old. Two of the smaller ones on our port beam hover, noses only inches apart, waving a front flipper each, for all the world like two gossips exchanging the latest news. We have never seen turtles en masse like this before; only the occasional solitary one, raising its head once, for a breath of air and a look around, then not to be seen again however long you keep looking.

There is something of the turtle about us, come to think of it. Our pace is leisurely. We are vulnerable to gales and strong currents and we carry our home with us wherever we go. Our journeys are usually solitary although we do occasionally meet up with our own kind at marinas and town quays and have a gossip. But with such a vast territory in which to roam, we rarely meet up with the same people twice. This time last year, wary of our capabilities and all too aware of our inexperience, we were more akin to the dolphin—rapid in our movements, darting and diving, a little edgy. Watching the pod for confirmation. But twelve months on we have settled into our new world and in pace, rhythm and restful solitude this is our summer of the turtle.

For some reason the flotilla currently making its way down our sides makes me think of the mass migration of yachtsmen that takes place every year, as hundreds of boats embark on an Atlantic crossing to that ultimate in warm blue waters, the Caribbean. It is a migration in which, this coming autumn, we plan to take part.

THE PRESENT JOURNEY TO Sardinia will take around thirty hours and this is a lazy sort of day for doing whatever you fancy. During the daytime at sea we don't keep a formal watch. Apart from the time spent in the galley or at the chart table by one of us, we are both out in the cockpit anyway so keeping a lookout is not arduous. With one of us up in the helmsman's chair facing for'ard and the other one propped against the cockpit cushions pointing astern, we only have to look up from our books and turn our heads to cover a 360° radius between us. Only after our evening meal, with night approaching and one of us below, do we keep a dedicated watch.

When we first set out we kept a three-hour watch but found that if the person getting up and into warm clothing was slow off the mark, the one retiring sometimes got only two-and-a-half hours rest. So we tried a four-hour watch, which was better for the person sleeping, but proved too long for the person on watch. So now we do three-and-a-half, using the half hour as a change-over period.

I take the first one, from 8.30pm until midnight. At 9pm there is a stunning orange sky as a huge golden sun changes to red just before it sinks. By eleven the sky is ablaze with stars. An enormous red moon appears. As it rises it turns deep yellow with pink edges then gradually fades to palest gold. I can see its craters clearly.

I see no other boats all night, although on David's watch there is one, a tanker, and we are on a collision course with it. Only one other vessel in ten hours in a whole sea and we are on a collision course with it. This is not, of course, surprising when you think about it. Set the GPS to get you from point A to point B and inevitably anyone traveling in the opposite direction will be on the same course as you. This is one of the reasons why you keep a watch.

Potential collisions apart, I wonder sometimes whether I ever really looked at things before. On land there are so many distractions. Alone on an empty sea the eye looks longer and with a more concentrated gaze at whatever turns up. The very absence of stimuli much of the time makes an appearance, when it does come, so much more vivid: whether it is unexpected, like the sudden arrival of turtles; or anticipated, like the return of the sun after a dark night.

LOW CLOUD ON THE eastern horizon obscures the sun's rise next morning. When it does begin to force its way through, its radiance is fragmented as if red-hot embers are burning holes in the cloud. When it does finally emerge, it changes from deepest red to butter yellow and hangs above our port bow. At the same time, a gauzy moon glows dull silver over our starboard quarter while Venus, the last star left in the sky, descends into the sea.

By 9.30 we are far enough into Italian waters to tune in to Channel 68 on the VHF and hear the Italian weather forecast. It will be a great relief to be able to get a forecast on demand, despite the fact that this first one bears no relation to present conditions nor to those we are destined to encounter in a few hours time; but then, the Italian authorities cannot be held responsible for the unpredictability of this summer's weather.

The Italian weather broadcasting system provides a 24-hours-a-day continuous forecast alternately in Italian and in English and delivered in such a way that it is audible even in difficult conditions. Despite being computerized for clarity and consistency, the result is a rich baritone voice with overtones of warm brandy and cigar smoke that resonates through the VHF speaker, slowly and distinctly, so that even the Italian words are easily identifiable to an English ear. There is no verbiage to clutter up the vital core information either, or to cause confusion as to actual meaning. But if you should miss anything, all you have to do is stay tuned and the bit you missed will ultimately come round again. If you are listening in English you will of course have to wait for the Italian version to pass, but since the broadcast follows a very simple formula which is the same in both languages, with a brief jaunt through the meteorological pages of the Cruising Association's invaluable *Yachtsman's Ten Language Dictionary* you can usually get the bit of the broadcast you want from the Italian part without waiting for the English to come round again.

The simple formula consists of a category such as visibility (*visibilita*), wind (*vento*) or sea state (*mare*) followed by a description such as fair (*discreto*), decreasing (*diminuzione*) or slight (*poco mosso*). It is not only supremely practical but also quite beautiful. Each Italian word, with its rolling Rs and every syllable given due weight, becomes a series of musical notes played on a cello. I am captivated.

'I've already got the forecast,' David will call from the cockpit as I tune in to Channel 68 yet again. And I sink back into the cushions, close my eyes and sigh as the slow, dark, fruity voice transforms a mundane shipping forecast into rhythmic, hypnotic sound. *Visibilita: discreto. Vento: diminuzione. Mare: poco mosso. Lentamente* (slowly). *Sereno* (clear sky). *Nuvoloso.* I particularly like the pulsating roundness of *nuvoloso*, even if it does mean 'cloudy'.

AT 11.30AM WE SPOT what initially looks like a group of large birds on the water ahead of us flapping their wings. It is noteworthy because in nearly 24 hours we have seen no birds at all. As we get closer it becomes apparent that they are fins. It is a family of bottlenose dolphins and they come leaping to our bow like school kids at a new prospect in the playground. There are eight of them, although two stand out because one is larger and paler than the rest and the other smaller and darker. While the remainder of the group take turns to swim ahead of our bows or dive under them, these two embark on some synchronized swimming between our hulls. Then they go freestyle and arc, dive, roll over each other and dodge back and forth between the inside and outside of the hulls. Having exhausted their repertoire, and like the turtles of the previous day, they set off in a westerly direction towards Menorca.

Within an hour there are even more turtles trundling down our hulls than yesterday, all heading west, with David grumbling that they do not seem to understand the International Collision Avoidance Regulations about passing port-to-port. Mainland Italy has a reputation among visiting yachtsmen for officious officials, homicidal fishermen, and men with violin cases demanding money with menaces for a brief stop at a supposedly-free public quay. Someone who sailed Italy regularly explained the last-mentioned thus: the local mafia, he said, 'sells' a section of the dock and the 'buyer' makes as much money out of it from visiting boats as he can. But none of that can explain why its marine life appears to be emigrating to Spain.

17

The Sinis Peninsula

After Sicily, Sardinia is the largest island in the Mediterranean. Although Italian, Sardinia is quite different from mainland Italy thanks to its geographical position—halfway between Europe and Africa—and the various civilizations which have left their mark on it. The earliest known was a native culture called Nuraghic, after the thousands of *nuraghe*—stone constructions built between 1500 and 500BC for housing the living and the dead—to be found all over the island. The Phoenicians traded and settled here. The Carthaginians, whose capital lay only 150 miles away on the North African coast near modern-day Tunis, then settled on the island until overwhelmed by the Romans in 176 BC with a massive loss of life among the islanders.

After the fall of Rome in the 5th century AD, a combination of barbarian incursions, malaria and five centuries of Muslim raids continued to reduce the island's population and even today it still has little in the way of large cities or heavy industry. The medieval city-states of Pisa and Genoa fought over parts of it, while in 1297 Pope Boniface VIII gave all of it to Spain in exchange for abandoning its claims to Sicily. Following the War of the Spanish Succession (1701-20), Sardinia was ceded first to Austria and then to the Duke of Savoy. Since the Unification of Italy, in 1861, the island has been part of Italy.

We arrive on its eastern side at mid-afternoon, 32 hours after leaving Menorca, and settle in the small exposed anchorage of Capo San Marco off the Sinis Peninsula. The water is incredibly clear and the line of our anchor chain is visible in the sand all along its length thirteen feet below us. Our thermometer says 94°F. It is of the old-fashioned type with a glass phial of red liquid and it lies in the shady recesses of a cockpit cubby-hole. It is an English one and accordingly only goes up to 115°F on the principle that human life would become extinct beyond that anyway.

Some small pleasure-boat owners and a couple of divers come out to have a look at us. Sardinians do it differently from the Spanish. The latter will observe and discuss your boat among themselves but not make eye contact unless you initiate it. Sardinians look directly at you, and when you smile, their faces light up and they wave and it all becomes very sociable. Unless, of course, they are wearing uniforms.

THE SENIOR OF THE two Carabinieri officers in the boat that arrives alongside ours rests his hand on the black leather holster on his right hip. 'You have one of these?'

'No!' says David.

He's never been asked about guns before. Not even during his multiple-interrogation by Portuguese customs, police, port authority and marina personnel.

'A Very pistol?' he persists, convinced we must have *something* resembling a weapon.

'No,' says David. 'Only hand-held flares.'

Unconvinced, the officer carries our ship's papers, passports and insurance certificate below to record their details. His subordinate holds their green and white motor launch steady against Voyager and stares over our heads. David sighs. Italian bureaucracy is notorious and at such times there is always the fear that if an official gets it into his head that you have something illegal on board—or simply doesn't like the look of you—he can impound your boat *and take it apart*. Even drilling holes in all the bulkheads to look for hidden compartments is not unknown.

In the longueur that follows, my glance falls on the copy of a tourist guide to Italy that I have been reading. Both the tourist guide and our cruising guide mention Tharros, the remains of a city variously described as Phoenician, Carthaginian or Punic Roman. I very much want to see it but neither book gives its exact location, nor is it marked on our chart. In the present heat I do not have the energy to waste wandering miles in the wrong direction through deserted hills.

I pick up the guide, left open at the page with Tharros mentioned on it and look across at David. 'Shall I ask him?' I say.

'If you like,' David replies, without enthusiasm.

'Signore …' I venture. I'm always terrified of mispronouncing the final vowel of the word and unwittingly calling an Italian man 'Madam'. The two words are so dangerously alike and in the present circumstances such a slip could be disastrous. 'Signore… Tharros, per piacere. Is it far?' I am keeping to the bare essentials, albeit politely.

He stops scrutinizing the sky and lowers his head slowly until his eyes are level with mine. I interpret his lack of response as the fault of my pronunciation. I decide to cut to the barest essential of all.

'Tharros?' I repeat, politely.

Somewhere behind his very dark glasses I think he may have blinked. I hold the book towards him, open at the relevant page. He makes no move to take it. I point to the word, standing out in bold letters, adding helpfully, 'Phoenician.'

He glances at the page for a nanosecond then contemplates me again.

'*T*arros' he corrects, dropping the 'h'. Then, looking over the top of his sunglasses with utter contempt, he snaps, 'Carthaginian!'

The other officer re-emerges and returns our documents. His demeanor has changed. Whether our passports have reassured him that married fifty-somethings are unlikely drug smugglers, or our insurance certificate has confirmed that we are not going to be a financial liability we shall never know. Maybe he is simply pleased at our interest in his heritage for he points east and says, 'About a mile.'

We thank him. He turns away but as his partner revs their engine he hesitates and looks back.

'You stay here?' he asks, indicating the little bay and beach.

'Ye-es?' says David, expecting to be told an overnight stay is not allowed.

'Next bay,' he says. 'Better.'

And so it turns out.

Before we can set off for it, however, a second green and white power boat with two officials in it heads towards us. This one says *Guardia Civil* on the side. David, head first into the big stern locker looking for something, has his back towards it.

'David,' I say, 'who's top dog in Italian officialdom: Carabinieri or Guardia Civil?'

Before he can answer, a hand clamps onto our rail and a pair of very dark sunglasses focus on me. The officer behind them is young and *very* cocky. I can already see the sawdust rising as an electric drill grinds its way through my few cherished bits of polished wood paneling.

'Peppers!' he snaps.

His boat is smaller and his uniform less impressive than his predecessors, so I take a punt.

'OK,' I say rising from my seat. 'But the Carabinieri had them not 10 minutes ago.'

His hand flies from our rail as if it has suddenly become red-hot.

I have reached the companionway doors. 'I'll get them.'

'No!' he says, backing away and waving a restraining hand. 'No, no. Is okay. S'okay. Bi-bi.'

Their boat roars away. David backs out from the stern locker and straightens up. 'Carabinieri,' he says.

Fortunately, the only other uniform we encounter during our stay in Sardinia is on the public quay at the island's capital, Cagliari. Immaculate, epauletted and very formal in demeanor, we assume they are port authority officials and nod respectfully whenever they stroll past inspecting the boats. Only just before we leave will we discover that they are car park attendants.

THE BAY JUST AROUND the headland which the Carabinieri officer has recommended turns out to be a much more sheltered anchorage than our initial one. It is also Tharros. We have a perfect view of it from our cockpit. The ruined city tumbles down a low hill to the water's edge: citadel, public baths, houses, roads, temple and amphitheatre.

The Sinis Peninsula had been settled by the Phoenicians around 800 BC. Tharros was later occupied and developed by refugees from Carthage fleeing Rome's destruction of their own city during the Punic Wars. Tharros was ultimately absorbed into the Roman Empire just as surely as Carthage had been and the Romans expanded the city, also adding a temple and a theatre. The site's most prominent feature now is two Corinthian columns which is all that remains standing of the temple, built around the first century BC.

You get ashore at the adjacent village of San Giovanni di Sinis. After tying up the dinghy at a tiny wooden jetty almost hidden among the reeds the first dwellings you see are made from rushes, walls and roofs. Once fishermen's houses, they are now holiday homes. The village itself has a church dating from the fifth century. It is simple, cruciform, domed and windowless. It is blissfully cool inside and even on this witheringly hot day manages to smell slightly of damp. The sunlight streaming through its doorway illuminates the unadorned walls, the dome of its small interior and a young priest on his knees before the altar. He is wearing a white baseball cap back-to-front and his cassock tucked up into his belt as he beavers away with a dustpan and brush. The rising dust particles form a shimmering aureole around his head. Wednesday is cleaning day.

The village also contains several bars, a public telephone and a vast quantity of flies—a persistent problem with reed beds—but no shop. We have a cold beer at a bar on the beach. Several mothers and young children are running along the sand oblivious of the blistering heat. Our waitress appears to be in the later stages of exhaustion.

In the evening, after dinner, we sit in our cockpit and reflect that where we are anchored the Phoenicians, among the ancient world's greatest sailors, had anchored their ships. Our steel anchor and chain is lying on the seabed where their stone and rope anchors once lay. Voyager must constantly have rested where the boats of ancient peoples had. But on this glorious evening, with an enormous red sun setting behind the old city's two Corinthian columns, we are more sensible of all the lives that have gone before us than at any time before or since.

18

Torre Grande

....

Next morning the information on Navtex, the international weather forecasting and navigational warning system above our chart table, is varied and plentiful. A Swedish boat is overdue between Alicante and Toulon; there is an oceanographic survey in the Adriatic; a gunnery exercise on the Azores coast; a dead black and white cow adrift off Corsica; and a light-buoy is operating on reduced power in the Dover Strait. For Sardinia, however, there is nothing, least of all a weather forecast.

Monaco Radio gives its English version only in the mornings and is often so fast and guttural that it is little more intelligible than the French. It is also not broadcast until 9am, which is too late in the day if you want to make a long passage. However, on VHF Channel 68 we have the wonderful, rolling 24-hours-a-day forecast in English and Italian, with that sonorous baritone voice speaking each word slowly and distinctly so that even with major static it is still audible.

Until I went sailing I thought one weather forecast said it all. In reality, it is only someone's interpretation of the raw data available. Listening to more than one can sometimes be confusing but more often than not you get a better picture of what is happening over time.

We get a VHF forecast for moderate breezes from an easterly direction and set out at seven o'clock for Carloforte, the only town on the Isola di S Pietro, an island lying off the south-western tip of Sardinia and named, like so many places where fishing is or was the major industry, after St Peter the patron saint of fishermen. It is a beautiful sunny day and promises a good sail. However, by 8am the moderate breezes have become strong ones and in no time reach near gale force. The journey to Carloforte will take about nine hours and it seems foolhardy to continue in a wind which is rapidly approaching gale force. It is also extremely uncomfortable with the sea banging against our beam. The sensible thing to do is turn back and head for somewhere sheltered.

Last night's anchorage, off Tharros, will be too exposed in this wind so we head for nearby Porto Oristano, a commercial harbor in which our cruising guide says we can anchor in safety. By the time we approach it the wind has dropped to 8mph and we feel we should really set out again, but we distrust this unsettled weather.

When we get inside the harbor things have clearly changed since the guide was published. There isn't a single yacht in it, only commercial boats tied up to the quays. We don't feel safe anchoring in such a rundown commercial area and decide to go over to a new marina near Torre Grande.

By the time we have tied up to a pontoon there is hardly any wind at all and we feel like wimps. The thermometer in the shade of the cockpit cubby hole registers 96°F. During the afternoon the wind rises steadily to the lower 30s but does nothing to reduce the heat. When I reach into the cockpit cubby hole for a pen my hand emerges with a red stain on it. I search for a cut but, despite fragments of glass in the cubby hole, there is none. The thermometer has accidentally become exposed to direct sunlight and its glass vial has exploded, spilling its red dye. The only other thermometer on board is an Age Concern cardboard one. Its concern is with hypothermia among the elderly and the appropriate use of heating fuel and only goes up to 80°F. On the other hand, it is probably better we don't know what the temperature really is at present.

SARDINIA HAS TRADITIONALLY BEEN a summer playground for foreign visitors and especially for its wealthier countrymen from the Italian mainland. By early evening a rush of boats returning from the nearby beaches gives an opportunity to observe a rather excitable example of the latter in action.

A 30ft yacht arrives at the pontoon opposite with a man sitting casually at the tiller and two bikini-clad young women on the bow; a ratio of at least two bikini-clad young women per man being *de rigueur* on Italian yachts. Although the man noses towards the pontoon, the wind drives his boat sideways into a neighboring boat. He remains sitting at the tiller, shouting instructions, while the two women hurtle up and down the side deck fending off.

To help the two girls, a member of the marina staff leaps onto the neighboring boat to fend off in their place, while two other marina staff pass them a rope each to tie up the bow. Once the bows are tied, that will be half the problem solved. Unfortunately, the boat is now almost at right angles to the one next door, and the two girls heave and strain on the bow ropes with such desperate vigor that the one in the green bikini pops out of her top. Women do not go topless in Sardinia so this attracts quite a number of other male bystanders who don't do anything much except get under the feet of the three who are trying to help the two girls.

Meantime, their skipper bellows instructions continually from his seat at the tiller, which is too low for him to see what is going on at the front of his boat anyway. Why he is still sitting there holding a useless tiller, and not applying some muscle for'ard, is something only to be comprehended within the male Italian psyche. However, by hauling feverishly on a rope with one hand and holding down her top with the other, the girl in the green bikini manages to get her bow rope tied. What is needed now is for the lazy line to be attached to the boat's stern where it can be used to pull and hold the vessel parallel to its neighbor. Leaving her companion to struggle with the other bow rope, she hauls up the lazy line and begins walking down the side deck with it towards the man on the tiller who is still bawling instructions to nobody in particular.

For the first time in the whole process, though, he is now in the right place. All he has to do is wait for her to reach the stern, take the lazy line from her, haul on it until the boat is at right angles to the quay, and then tie it to the cleat at his feet. Instead, he gets up, walks towards her, whisks it majestically from her hand and begins hauling on it from amidships— which serves only to send the boat even further askew. He has also failed to check if the second bow rope has actually been tied off before he begins hauling on the lazy line. It hasn't, the boat having been blown too far sideways for the rope to reach a cleat and the two girls end up hanging onto it like grim death.

From our berth on the pontoon opposite, this now becomes a scene from Italian opera. There is one bow rope tied, but the boat is skewed at a drunken angle and a hazard to passing boats because its skipper (The Hero) is now pulling it *away* from the pontoon and defeating the combined efforts of both girls (The Heroine and her Trusty Maid) to tie the second rope. And an exhausted marina attendant (Faithful Manservant) is still bent double over the rails of the neighboring boat fending off the Hero's.

Meanwhile, at the back of the stage, a growing semi-circle of male extras (The Chorus) waits for the green bikini top to shoot skyward again.

Cue an aria. For an interminable length of time The Hero stands amidships, heaving on the lazy line, bawling his complaint to the heavens in a fine tenor voice, but futilely since in the best dramatic traditions he is the architect of his own downfall. Meantime, thanks to his latest efforts, his stern is in imminent danger of colliding with another boat two spaces down. In fact, his boat is now at such an angle that he is in danger of damaging *two* boats—one with his bow and one with his stern.

The Faithful Manservant finally persuades him to do what a man's gotta do and take the lazy line to the stern, which he does. But instead of tying it round a cleat when he gets there, he clutches it to his chest with both hands, leans back, legs braced, biceps throbbing, and howls his titanic lament to the heavens and an increasing wind like the tragic captain of a sinking ship.

I declare an interval and make a pot of tea. The plot has sunk into anti-climax. Then, just as I begin to despair of the denouement, the *deus ex machina* arrives in the form of another yacht. This one has two men and four bikini-clad women on it. They putter in, make a sharp left, fend off The Hero's stern as they nudge their way in beside him, tie up their bow, fasten their own lazy line and then hop over their rail and tie up his— making a total of twelve people berthing one 30ft boat. Then all the actors leave the stage, followed by The Chorus, to the sound of a rousing finale as The Hero loudly describes to his rescuers what a terrible time he's had and how he finally resolved it.

THE WIND ROARS ON into the night, slackens briefly around dawn and then picks up again. The disco in Torre Grande, a mile and a half away, ends at 4am. Nevertheless, we rise from a surprisingly refreshing night's sleep and cycle across the marina to pay our dues. It is unexpectedly expensive and we have to pedal back to the boat for more money to go shopping. We also collect our gash bag which we had forgotten to take with us.

As he approaches the open dumpster on our return run, David does a stylish swerve and hurls the bag. Only by yanking the handlebars at the last moment, however, does his front wheel miss the bottle bank and this spoils his aim. He dismounts, retrieves the gash bag from behind the dumpster and sheepishly drops it in. As he is always the first to admit, his large gestures are always doomed. But it never stops him.

My knees begin to give out half way to Torre Grande and I have to stop. What with unearthing the bicycles, pumping up their tires, my rest periods, and then putting the bikes away again afterwards it would probably have been quicker to walk. However, there is a sense of achievement.

TORRE GRANDE'S TINY SUPERMARKET is air-conditioned, extremely cold, cramped and packed with people. After cycling in the heat and then going into its extreme cold, something strange happens to our personal thermostats so that after ten minutes inside, and despite the chill, we stand at the checkout streaming with perspiration.

Outside again we have a cold beer at a pavement café and then cycle down a side street leading to the promenade. A three-wheel Piagio truck with a small motorcycle engine wobbles towards us. In its one-seater cab two beefy men sit side by side, like sardines wedged into a can. By the intense expressions on their faces, steering is a bit of a problem.

We turn right onto the promenade, which is for pedestrians only and has a policeman on duty, but we cycle slowly and carefully and smile as we pass him for we have discovered that most things are achievable if you have grey hair and smile nicely.

I make it back to the marina without a rest, thanks to a following wind and a slight downward slope to the road. The beer probably helped as well. We have a lovely lunch of hard Spanish cheese, Italian bread, a local pastry like a jam tart and coffee on our *terrace*, as I've taken to calling our cockpit since an enormous Italian power boat arrived next door. What else can you call something with patio doors and large terracotta pots with shrubs in them *except* a terrace? David accuses me of being a closet motor yacht owner.

Our neighbors on the other side are Austrian. They always look particularly neat and well pressed although their sloop is very small and spartan. They ask us if we have a forecast, as the one in the marina window is a week old and they do not have a shortwave radio. We say we will try to get Radio Monaco at 7.15 this evening. They look pleased and we start work on a variety of chores.

As soon as you have access to a tap you do all the jobs that require lots of water. I do some laundry, and use lime de-scaler on the steam iron which no longer steams, and on our electric kettle which has been taking 10 minutes to boil two cups of water. David investigates a water leak in the starboard engine bay and we both have baths. Then we set about refilling our port tank. We test the water beforehand. We hold a glass of it up to the light, sniff it, sip it, consider it and pronounce it quite palatable. Just as the tank booms full, however, a passing Italian waves an anxious hand at the hose in our tank and cries, 'Not potable!' He goes on to explain that the only drinking water comes from a single tap on the far end of the quay. The water from all the other taps is fit only for washing boats.

It is important that you always ask somebody relevant if the water on tap is safe to drink *before* you fill your tank with it, even if it seems OK. We knew that, but had become careless. It is fortunate that only one tank needed filling. The other contains good water we brought with us. Rather than go to all the trouble of emptying the tank we have just filled, we decide to use the non-potable tank for baths and washing up, and the other one for drinking and cooking. By now it is 7.45pm and we've missed the 7.15 Monaco weather forecast for our Austrian neighbors. The one at nine tomorrow morning will be too late for them, but we say they will probably be as well off with Channel 68 on the VHF anyway. It is then we discover that they don't have a VHF radio either, which is pretty basic sailing in open waters, so we tune into Ch 68 for them.

19

Torre Grande to Carloforte

....

We get up early next morning, having decided to empty the port tank and refill it with potable water after all. Swapping between two tanks would become a pain and leave the plumbing tainted anyway. We compare the Monaco and Italian forecasts. Conditions will probably be quite bad tomorrow, though not too bad today. It is worth making a run for Carloforte, 48 miles down the coast, to get further south and hopefully away from the bad weather. Before we leave, we go to the end of the quay to fill up with water, and then round to the fuel dock where a fisherman very generously abandons his own boat at another pump to come and help tie up ours.

Out in the bay someone has obviously been seeing just how many red marker buoys and other obstacles they can scatter about on a morning that quickly becomes so misty we have to put on our radar. We cut the corner of the *Zone Prohibito*—fortunately the Military is not doing any target practice there this morning—and pick our way through a minefield of fishing buoys. We have delicious Italian bread and ham for lunch. Then afterwards, with Voyager all alone and private, I abandon my swim suit so the sun can reach those parts it is rarely privy to.

By 5pm, with the wind now northerly, the afternoon has grown cooler. I have one leg back in my swim suit, and the other just entering, when there is a tremendous roar. It is a sound I recognize. I yank the straps over my shoulders and turn to see a jet fighter at eye level a quarter of a mile off our starboard side.

I am familiar with jet fighter planes, having once lived in an area where the Royal Air Force practiced low-level flying. Walking our dogs along the top of the hills above our home, I would spot a black dot on the horizon and brace myself for the inevitable. You *could* make a run for it, but risked injury tumbling down a steep slope if you tried a vertical escape, and the drop of a few yards made no reduction in the decibel level anyway. Sprinting along the ridge to avoid the plane was also futile. The pilot simply adjusted his steering a fraction and got you anyway.

Anyone up there was his prey and his intention was to pass directly over your head. He had homed in on you from another range of hills miles away across the valley and did not intend that you should escape. So you simply put your hands over your ears and waited for the pain to stop. The poor dogs didn't have that option, of course. The pilots enjoyed it, though. I know because they twinkled their lights on the plane's undercarriage to signal their satisfaction as they passed over my upturned face. And once, one of them was so close that I could see someone inside the cockpit smiling.

Being targeted down in the valley was even worse than up on the hills. At least on the hills you could see the plane coming. Down on the field paths, or in the village park, you were unaware of its presence until it came over the treetops at you. Then, just when you thought you might be having a heart attack from the sudden shock, the sound would hit you.

But what is a little hearing impairment—or two anxious dogs who constantly bump into things because they are always watching the sky—compared to doing one's bit for national security and international prestige? By providing a moving target in an otherwise static landscape I was enabling Britain's fighter pilots to become second-to-none at low-level flying. And low level flying we are told is essential in reducing collateral damage. Having completed many involuntary tours of duty with the RAF in my younger days, however, I think it unfair of Italy's Air Force to now expect me to provide a similar service for them. At my age. And in my present state of *dishabille*.

As the Italian pilot hurtles towards us my eardrums recall every agonizing decibel of a jet fighter engine at close quarters. He is almost upon us when he climbs vertically and spirals away, leaving behind him a thick column of black smoke with us at the bottom of it: deafened, coughing and groping for handholds since, like the sound, it is only after the plane disappears that its air turbulence strikes you. For a few moments it is like being hit by an unheralded gale on the beam with all the sails up. It's a thankless task, training fighter pilots.

MEANWHILE, WITH THE WIND coming from the north it is now almost directly onto our stern. It begins to increase and, with a moderate sea, we begin to surf at speed. Catamarans excel with the wind behind them, giving a smooth, fast sail. With both the wind and the sea coming from behind, Voyager is flying along. The wind speed indicator is showing only 19mph of wind and I fail to add the boat speed to it to give a true wind speed. Because it is so peaceful on board, without resistance to wind or water, it is a shock when we turn right into the channel for Carloforte Harbor and encounter the rattle and turbulence of a 30mph wind on our beam.

Most of the navigation buoys shown in the cruising guide have disappeared, but when we turn into the wind and spray to take in the genoa we still manage to end up heading at speed for one of the few that remain. We miss it, fortunately, and head with relief for the harbor and marina. It is shallow in the channel, and the sandy patches shine bright aquamarine among the dark weed. I tie on ropes and fenders and at 6.30pm we approach the yacht club marina, only to be waved away towards the sea wall.

Those already tied up to it are anxiously staring at their fenders being crushed against the wall by the force of the wind, and one yachtsman is even putting out an anchor to try and hold his boat off it. So we anchor out instead, listen to the forecasts, and drink a glass of wine while I prepare square Spanish spaghetti and a Bolognese sauce, with a red kidney bean and olive salad to have with the Italian bread.

CARLOFORTE HAS A VERY pretty waterfront of tall elegant houses all in different pastel colors, lots of trees and a boulevard of tall palms. If anything it is almost prettier at dusk. Unlike most promenades with their long strings of white, uniform electric lights, here each street lamp has three round globes set at different heights. With their soft golden light, the trees dark against the pastel buildings, the occasional yellow rectangle of a lighted window and the lush wooded hills in the background, there is endless variety and enjoyment for the eye.

It is also a busy harbor. Sarena ferries arrive and depart half-hourly until sunset and there are a lot of yachts at anchor from many nations. We have an Irish motor yacht behind us, a small dark blue Australian sloop on our port side, a Finnish ketch to starboard and a Danish sloop in front. We have settled a little closer to the Australian sloop than we should have liked but the anchor has set firmly and we are loath to raise it again. With the wind maintaining 30mph, however, we share an anchor watch. We are anxious that if we and the Aussie yacht swing out of sync we might collide and, surrounded as we are, if we began to drag we should inevitably hit another boat. Happily, the little Australian sloop sits out the wind-tossed, anchor-wrenching night like a plank, and so do we. Not so the Danish boat which dances all night, and an American boat whose owner gives up the struggle with the sea wall in the early hours and anchors not far from us.

20

Carloforte

A fter a rather bumpy trip ashore next morning we tie our dinghy to
a pontoon in an area which the yacht club marina uses for small local boats. A young man appears and indicates the almost empty pontoon
regretfully. Our mooring there, he explains, is causing him a lot of problems. He doesn't quite have his hand out, so we keep ours in our pockets.
'We have no food,' we say. 'Only be an hour.'

The big *supermercato* is at one end of the harbor while the post office—
a nice man explains very apologetically—is 'at the other end of town, up
the hill, turn right, keep going, turn left and keep going, left then right …
a long way.' It is around 11am and getting hot, and with concerns about
our dinghy we decide to concentrate on the supermarket.

A small boy outside, hand extended, smiles angelically at us and we
give him our 500 lire coin in exchange for his shopping cart rather than
wrestle to free one from a nearby chain gang. Clutching the coin he disappears like smoke in a Force 9 and we discover the cart has a dud mecha-
nism and no coin in it. It also has a wobbly wheel, but we don't have
another 500 lire coin to enable us to unchain a better one. We spend a
small fortune inside the store and stagger back to the waterfront loaded
down with fresh meat, fish, fruit and vegetables and what turn out to be
some very tasty little pizzas.

Changing countries means changing language and currency. Having
finally reached a state of basic communication and courtesy in Spain, despite our best efforts otherwise we are now talking Spanish to Italians.
And whereas Spain has around 200 pesetas to the £sterling and the shops
never have enough small change, here you end up with pockets full of it as

there are currently around 2,800 lire to the £sterling and the largest coin is only 500 lire. Whenever the final coin needed for your change is of an infinitesimal value they give you a wrapped sweet instead, although they do not accept these back again as legal tender.

At the quay we are greeted by two women from the American yacht that anchored near Voyager during the night, and we ask if they know where we can leave a dinghy without hassle. They point out a trawler against the quay and say he is a yacht-friendly fisherman who lets you tie your dinghy to his boat. 'Everyone else wants your cash,' they say. It is interesting that we all accept that if we drove a car into the town we would have to pay to park it. Yet as no other country charges yachtsmen to leave a dinghy, we all feel affronted; or afraid, perhaps, that the habit might spread.

On our way back down the yacht club marina's main pontoon to retrieve our dinghy we notice a British yacht, mainly because on its stern, sitting straddle-legged over a bucket, a classic sea dog with grizzled hair and beard is washing his Y-fronts. He looks up at us and our supermarket polybags. We look down at his laundry. 'Ahh,' I breathe, 'the sheer romance of sailing.' Laughing makes him cough, but when he stops he introduces himself as Toby. His wife Lyn emerges from the galley to introduce herself. They will be heading for Cagliari shortly and we will encounter them again.

Back on board Voyager we observe Boudicca going ashore. She is a matron from a British yacht called Steadfast or Sedulous, or something of that sort, whom we have seen in several Spanish anchorages. Her male companion sits in the stern of their red rubber dinghy and steers while she stands in its bow, gripping the painter like the ancient British heroine leading the charge against the Roman invaders. It is rather choppy for standing today and takes even more grim determination than usual.

With bad weather predicted for tomorrow there are quite a few new arrivals seeking shelter. Like us, observing empty berths on the pontoons ahead of them, each one sweeps determinedly towards the yacht club marina and is just as determinedly waved away. Among them is a French yacht with two white-haired men aboard who then have an awful time anchoring. They arrive at their chosen spot too fast, drop their anchor too soon, travel over the top of it, let out too little chain, drag, heave the anchor back on board and try somewhere else. Inevitably, as they struggle, the wind rises to its daily peak and they look wretched as each new attempt to get their anchor down fails. The people closest keep shouting to them to let out more chain. Unfortunately, with the language barrier and the strength of the wind, they simply raise their anchor and move on again.

Meanwhile, two little girls in an Optimist sailing dinghy return, sopping wet and whooping with so much excitement from the challenging conditions beyond the harbor wall that they almost collide with the two struggling Frenchmen. Finally the French yacht moves closer to the quay where it is shallow enough for the small amount of chain being let out to let the anchor bite.

21

A Quiet Day In

The weather forecast next day is still unsuitable for moving further along the coast, and the sea state within the harbor is too rough for a dinghy ride ashore. So we stay aboard. We have everything we need. And there is never a shortage of things waiting to be done.

In the process of regaining some sort of control over our workshop and storage area David finds our Cruising Association and Royal National Lifeboat Institute pennants. They were laundered some time ago but have been missing ever since. He now hoists them aloft on the portside lanyard. Then, with a selection of charts and cruising guides, he settles on the sofa in the bow to prepare ahead.

Meanwhile I set about washing and preparing the wealth of vegetables bought yesterday to make ratatouille. I use whatever vegetables are available that we like: onions, peppers, carrots, garlic, tomatoes, beans, zucchini, squash, aubergine, mushrooms, celery, beans, broccoli. It makes a very tasty accompaniment to meat or fish. It is also very convenient, when you are at sea or anchoring late, to have a vegetable course that simply needs reheating, or an instant base for a casserole or pasta sauce. And you can always cut up the vegetables with kitchen scissors, add more stock and have instant home-made soup.

On a boat people tend do the things they like doing and the things that come easily to them. Whatever is left over has to be negotiated. David services the engines, but we share the routine maintenance. I do all the varnishing but David does all the sanding down beforehand. David enjoys navigation and planning. If I had to do it, we should still be living in a house. But I do enjoy cooking, especially when I can do the preparatory work sitting at the cockpit table in the sunshine with the radio tuned to BBC World Service and a glass of wine handy.

David does more than his share of the washing up—he says it appeals to his sense of order—and breakfast, and quite often our third meal of the day as well; apart from any accompanying salad which he finds finicky, but which I don't mind doing. At the same time he will happily produce an equally finicky fresh fruit salad, the preparation of which bores me to distraction. The truth is, I like salad with a meal and he likes fruit afterwards. Neither of us would bother with the other if it wasn't put in front of us, but we enjoy it when it is, and it means we get the recommended amount of healthful fruit and vegetables most days of the week.

David will happily spend hours at the helm. My concentration drifts after a while. He takes us onto pontoons in bad weather because he's good at it and I'm faster at tying up. If Voyager is plugged into the mains, he will vacuum the carpets to save my back and hands. If it's a dust pan and brush job I do it to save his sinuses.

As it turns out, not much navigation and planning gets done today. There is too much going on outside the bow windows. For instance, tension mounts over on the sea wall when a black-hulled 26-footer unfurls a German ensign that is at least 10 feet square. A white-hulled 28-footer, three boats along from it, puts out an enormous French ensign. There is also some shouting.

Surprisingly, given the weather, the Irish motor yacht leaves the harbor and the dancing Dane moves into its space. When the Irish boat returns soon after, its skipper has to find a new space in which to lower its anchor. The young couple who do the work, in their neat white polo shirts and navy shorts, we decide are professional crew while the two sulky adolescents they ferry back and forth into town in a RIB, and wait on, and who take no interest whatever in the yacht or their surroundings, look like owner's children in need of parental attention. The skipper has trouble getting his anchor to bite, and spends ages fretting over it. We wonder if, like Colin, he and his wife spend their time in a tiny windowless cabin in between their boat duties and waiting on the two brats. When the boat is finally settled to their satisfaction they begin washing it.

Just when everybody seems settled, the skipper of the dancing Danish yacht lifts his anchor again and attempts to lay it in the ferry lane. He is visited by three official-looking men in a RIB who tell him he can't, and he finally settles across the harbor near the children's swimming pool where the boat dances into the night.

When a red-hulled schooner enters the harbor and heads for the marina, at speed and with all its fenders flying, everybody it passes waves and shouts that it won't be allowed in. To everyone's surprise, it is. Either its skipper is a member of the yacht club or else the marina attendant has no choice when the schooner lands on the pontoon's windward side with 30mph of wind behind it. By now the sulky siblings on the Irish motor yacht have been fed and the boat is being polished.

All this and more keeps David from his charts and his nose against the bow window, with the odd bit of commentary to me. It never fails to surprise me how long it actually takes to produce simple dishes. The ratatouille has taken an hour and a half today from first slice of the onions to finally putting the lid on the pan. Unfortunately, having just produced a substantial quantity, which will need to be stored in the refrigerator, we now suspect we are getting low on propane.

WE HAVE SOME OF the ratatouille with trout and potatoes for dinner, followed by fresh peaches and kiwi fruit, and the last couple of squares of the last-but-one slab of chocolate truffle from Mahon—which also needs to be kept in the refrigerator. As we savor it with our coffee we wonder when we shall taste its like again.

When it comes time to turn in for the night we become aware of a strange noise. Usually the culprit is the boom, which under certain conditions can vibrate like a plucked double bass, sending a sonorous thrumming via the mast down through the boat. It only ever seems to occur at night, normally just after you have got into bed, but is so insistent that you've no chance of going to sleep until you go outside and stop it. Tonight, however, the boom is innocent. And the sound is not so much the deep notes of a double bass as the high-pitched twanging of a jew's-harp.

After standing around on deck listening for some time, with a brisk wind taking liberties with our night attire, it becomes apparent that the sound is coming from the mast itself. We stare and listen for ages—at the shrouds and backstays which lead *from* it, and the sheets from the sails which are joined *to* it—but can detect not the slightest tremor anywhere. I am becoming cold and irritable.

'It's almost … ' I struggle for the word which most clearly describes the rhythm. 'It's almost as if there's something … *flapping*.'

David looks suddenly guilty. And when I follow his gaze up the mast, there they dimly are, the small pennants of the Cruising Association and Royal National Lifeboat Institute which he had hoisted aloft this morning; their fluttering so slight as to be barely apparent, and yet noticeably in time with the maddening twanging going on below deck.

22

A Jaunt Ashore

··

Moving on is still out of the question next day but the water in the harbor is quieter so we go ashore. We go to a different pontoon this time. I ask an elderly, immaculate, world-weary, non-English-speaking man reading a newspaper in a small office full of sailing trophies if we can leave our dinghy against his quay for a few hours. He sighs, nods resignedly and returns to his newspaper. I am not game to ask him where the post office is in case he changes his mind.

Instead I accost an elderly boatman on the canal with my best 'Permesso, Signore...' who frowns at my question and then points in the direction of a very large and impressive blue and white, three-storey building. We narrowly avoid getting run over three times trying to cross a very busy road on a blind corner, only to discover when we get to it that the blue and white building bears a sign saying *Instituto Nautico*. We thought it had looked a bit big for a post office. So we accost a young man on another busy road, surrounded by frenetic motorists and with no provision for pedestrians, who puts his life at risk to patiently give us directions.

Sometime later, lost in a maze of streets, we approach a middle-aged man who gives us very precise instructions. Dutifully we go right and left and right and left but finally grind to a halt in confusion. He catches up with us in a large piazza and puts us on the right track again. Some time after that he pulls alongside us in a car, invites us to get in and drives us there.

It is a small, temporary-looking building hidden among modern apartment blocks and we realize that the elderly man on the canal did not send us to the Instituto Nautico because he knew no better, nor because he didn't care to help us. He had been pointing up into the hills *above* the

Instituto Nautico but had been overwhelmed by the problem of explaining how to get there. Clearly, by its distance from the town centre, a post office was a late arrival in Carloforte.

It is hot and airless inside, and there are four long lines stretching from the counter almost to the back wall. We stand at the end of one of them. Standing is not something I do well. Nothing seems to move and I have visions of us spending the day there. We are surrounded by young men and I try to get a look at the piece of paper one of them is holding. After a while I catch a glimpse and my fears are confirmed. It is Social Security Check Day.

'Permesso, Signore...' I begin and waive a postcard at the young man in the line beside us. He backs away, as if propositioned. Another young man behind him understands, smiles and points at an empty bit of unattended counter at the far end of the room. We go and stand at it with relief and someone arrives on the other side of the reinforced glass barrier. The gap between this barrier and the counter is too narrow to get four envelopes and two postcards through it all at once, but sliding them through one at a time you can feel a delicious chill against your fingers from the air-conditioning on the other side.

David says, 'D'you think they'd let us keep our ratatouille in there?'

A more important question is: would we ever find our way back up here to reclaim it? We're not even sure we can find our boat again.

Italy's stamps seem to be on a par with its coins—there are three times as many of them as is practical. In fact, you feel that the stamps must have been printed for a much earlier postal rate, before inflation overtook it, and it takes an age to post two birthday cards, two letters and two picture postcards. All six become dappled with multiple stamps, the postcards losing part of their addresses underneath them, and then each postage stamp gets a rubber stamp crashing down on it, plus another under the address of each envelope for luck. There isn't room on the postcards for this final flourish, however, without making them undeliverable and they escape this ultimate pummeling.

We emerge hot, sticky and bearing more small change than ever. Our next challenge is to find our way back to the waterfront. We get lost several times, but keep making our way downhill on the principle that we are bound to arrive at sea level sooner or later. Finally we do, of course, and with our shopping and postage now taken care of and our dinghy safe from intimidation, we are free to enjoy Carloforte.

Each building along the quay is different in style from its neighbor, as well as being painted in a different pastel color. The frontages are stucco and vaguely classical in decoration with their pilasters and pediments painted a lighter shade than the rest of the building. Promenade and piazza alike are shaded by tall palm trees and everywhere there are oleanders, with single and double flowers, in shades from almost red to palest pink, cream and white. What a legacy they leave to us, those people who plant the trees and shrubs that give pleasure to the eye and shade from the heat of the day.

The main street manages to be elegant while at the same time lived-in. Men sit cross-legged in doorways weaving baskets. In between fashionable shop windows, clothes-airers stand tidily against house fronts—the only place to catch the sun for those without gardens or balconies. And Europe, in the main, eschews the electric tumble dryer. Why use expensive power, when solar heat is free? There is bougainvillea and cactus, and all is very neat and tidy. Even the canine population, from tiny lapdogs to large hounds, have careful, watchful owners.

A STEEP FLIGHT OF steps rises to the old town, a maze of narrow streets and tiny whitewashed houses. Up here it is shady and cool. Mature ladies, all in black, stand at front doors opening directly onto the narrow streets, selling tomatoes grown in their tiny back gardens.

The little stone houses and cobbled streets of Carloforte's old town remind us vividly of the Cornish fishing village of St Ives, on England's south-west coast, where we spent holidays in the 1960s. And given their past history and present lifestyle their inhabitants probably have more in common with one another than with their own countrymen in Manchester or Milan. There is a theory current among some anthropologists that there is no such thing as race, only geography.

On the way back down, one wall of a long, steep, narrow alley is festooned with drying tablecloths and napkins. Turn left at the last napkin and there's a very swish-looking restaurant; and you are back down on the quay again.

When we left our northern Protestant homeland I was wary of offending southern Catholic sensitivities, by the way one dresses in public places or enters churches, or even in such matters as hanging out washing 'on the Sabbath', which was a heated issue in my childhood even among women who never went to church. Wherever we've traveled, however, the streets are likely to be festooned with the family's underpinnings any day of the week, a tourist's outfit has to be bizarre to attract a second look, many churches are locked even on Sundays and some supermarkets sell contraceptives at the checkout.

The island of Isola di San Pietro on which Carloforte stands has a fascinating coastline. Even if the cruising guide had failed to point this out, you would know from the picture postcards outside the local souvenir shops. Racks of cards in the squares and promenades of any town are a quick and useful guide to places you might want to visit. The postcards in Carloforte show a rugged coastline with wind-sculpted monoliths and intriguing caves. So, after leaving the harbor next day we do a circular sightseeing tour of the island and gaze at its cliffs, caves, coves and inlets.

23

Carloforte to Calasetta

After the bluster of the past few days the wind now is almost nothing, but Voyager on the move creates her own cooling breeze in an otherwise very hot day. By mid-afternoon we arrive at Calasetta on the north western tip of neighboring Isola di Sant' Antioco.

This was the site of the Carthaginians' first colony in Sardinia after their flight from the Roman invasion of Carthage, and claims to have been inhabited continuously for over two and a half thousand years. Despite its name it has not been an island for a similar length of time, being linked on its eastern side to Sardinia's mainland by a causeway begun by the Carthaginians and completed by the Romans.

It was into the port just below this causeway that Horatio Nelson's flagship, Vanguard, was brought shortly before the Battle of the Nile in 1798 to have some storm damage repaired. Writing to his wife, Nelson complained that because Sardinia had recently declared its neutrality in the French Revolutionary War, his men were not allowed ashore while his ship was being re-rigged.

Two hundred years later, just a few miles north of there at the little town of Calasetta, Sardinia is still making life difficult for British mariners. They have remodeled the harbor since our cruising guide was published. The quay against which visiting yachts once berthed has been taken over by the local ferries, and a new breakwater has been built through the anchorage to give the harbor better protection. What remains of the anchorage is now littered with private mooring buoys. We make two attempts to get an anchor to grip in a small patch of mud and weed. Both fail, and after seeing five yachts depart from the long sea wall below the town we decide to go and tie up there.

ITALIAN YACHTSMEN ARE TRUE originals when it comes to parking their boats. Shortly after we tie up, one of the five yachts returns. Two men on the sea wall grab its pulpit and wrestle to keep its bow off the quay. The boat's skipper leaps over his rail, rushes round between them and grabs it too. The impression given is one of extreme urgency. Then the three of them stand there gossiping for the next 20 minutes, holding the pulpit with one hand apiece with the boat at a 45° angle, the sails only half down and never a rope joined anywhere. They never do tie up. A second yacht arrives and tempts the first back out into the bay.

Spanish quays and sea walls are always crowded with anglers but they are invariably male. Here women anglers are prominent. One of them, fiftyish and quite stunning in a red and white dress with side slits and a pristine white baseball hat gives us a wide, welcoming smile. Another phenomenon not encountered before is married couples, fishing from adjacent canvas stools and companionably passing knife or bait to one another.

We go for a stroll into town. Apart from the anglers on the sea wall we seem to be the only people abroad. We have a beer overlooking the harbor and visit the local shop when it opens at 5pm. It is very small but not un-naturally, being Italian, it has all the things you want for Italian cooking that you don't get in Spain's corner shops, and what is more it has huge bottle-green sugar melons under a sign saying *Offerto*—reduced in price. I am very partial to sugar melon but never buy one nowadays because its weight is about equal to a week's groceries and lugging one over a mile back to the boat *with* a week's groceries is a major deterrent. However, this shop is so close to home that distance is not a consideration and being at a bargain price as well it is too good an opportunity to miss.

I also buy fish sticks, the fish market having long since emptied its trays, but on our way back we pop in to buy ice to bolster our fridge, which we now turn off at night to preserve the propane for cooking. We return to Voyager to prepare the evening meal—a big circle of meaty Italian sausage, potatoes and ratatouille, which is particularly tasty with some baked beans added to it. The melon, which still requires a few more days to reach a peak of perfection, currently fills one of the galley sinks. When buying the melon I had considered only its carriage and not its storage. There is no free cupboard space large enough to hold it and I dare not risk it getting loose on a moving boat. Like some mega canon ball, it would destroy everything in its path.

Around 8pm a fishing boat arrives and its skipper walks purposefully towards us. He looks like he is going to make us move. Unfortunately there isn't anywhere else to go in the harbor, and it is rather late now to go looking for an anchorage along the coast.

'Domani,' I say, hopefully pointing a finger towards the open sea to make it clear that we do not intend becoming a fixture here. 'We go tomorrow.' The man stares at me thoughtfully, gets us to move as close as possible to the small day boat in front of us and then ties up his boat behind us. Fifteen minutes later another fishing boat arrives behind him. Its skipper looks at us resentfully and an unintelligible conversation ensues with hands thrust vigorously and repeatedly skywards. We assume he is saying we must go, but when we look to the first skipper for clarification he says cheerfully, 'No problem'.

He and his crew unload lobsters in an assortment of plastic laundry baskets and what look like scrubbed emulsion paint containers, load up their cars and drive away. They return soon after, climb aboard their boat, start its engine and take it away. The second skipper, with very bad grace, then begins shouting at his two-man crew to haul his own boat up into the empty space behind us. David goes ashore and takes the bow rope, as much in the cause of self-preservation as good neighborliness, and rapidly ends up pulling against the two crewmen hauling at the stern. These men can't see how close their boat is to Voyager. Their skipper can but, in what seems to be an act of pure bloody-mindedness, continues to shout at them to keep coming forward until it is only moments before our dinghy and davits start to bend. With my feet still on our stern, but the rest of me at full stretch across our dinghy, I pit all my strength against the fishing boat's bow. They are very heavy, fishing boats, even medium-sized ones, and this is not a good angle at which to try and exert pressure. Between us, however, David and I manage to hold it at bay two inches from our dinghy.

'Domani,' I say, glaring up at the skipper. 'We go tomorrow.' For a moment he eyes me balefully, horizontal across our dinghy. Then he yells something back to his crew which finally makes them stop pushing. The trawler is tied up, still only two inches from our dinghy. This will make our exit in the morning worthy of Houdini, since fishing boats don't go out on Sundays and we are already almost on top of the small day boat in front of us. The skipper knows and relishes this. However, it is a relief that all the pushing, pulling, shouting and arm waving has stopped. The catch is unloaded and driven away.

We vaguely assume that the crew will return to move their boat elsewhere for the next one to unload, although we can't imagine why, as it is a long wall with enough space for half a dozen fishing boats, and we wonder how many times we will have to go through this performance and for how long into the night. It is only after the skipper from the second boat does not return to take his boat away, and other boats tie up and unload their catches until the sea wall is full to capacity and all the crews go home, that we realize that the first skipper had very generously moved his own boat so that we could remain for the night.

There is a most glorious sunset.

At around 10pm we stroll into town and wonder again where everybody is. It is Saturday night and the wide quay is deserted apart from a man at the bottom of some wide steps who is teaching his young daughter to play football. His wife looks on, proudly. We climb the steps, up to a large church surrounded by narrow streets. One of these leads to a square with a war memorial in the middle and the Smoking Ice café on one side. We have found where the townspeople go on a Saturday night.

The square is absolutely packed with people; promenading, sitting at tables eating *gelati* from large glass bowls, or simply standing around together and talking. They are mostly families, some large and extended, some young couples, and lots and lots of children, especially very small ones. It is always a surprise to see such young children out so late in southern Europe. Yet oddly, far from crying with tiredness and irritability as their northern cousins tend to do at such an hour, they are surprisingly cheerful. Even the odd group of adolescent boys, so often a disruptive element at gatherings at home, is good humored and smiling.

Only the noise is shocking. The sheer volume of so many voices trapped in a small square by tall houses is overwhelming. Clutching enormous ice-cream cones we make our way back down to the tranquility of the sea wall. There are almost as many anglers there now as during the day. One of them wears a miner's head lamp so that he can see to bait his hook throughout the night. Back on board, reaching for the light switch above the galley, I recoil at an unfamiliar shape in the darkness until I remember that there is an outsize sugar melon in the sink.

24

Calasetta to Malfatano

....

It is an almost windless morning, which is fortunate otherwise we should have to stay here until the fishing boat behind us goes to sea again on Monday. I push our stern out as far as my arms will reach and then haul myself up onto the bow as David reverses from the dock. It is indeed an escape worthy of a Houdini.

The forecast for the day is a moderate breeze from the west becoming east. Once out at sea the wind for the first half an hour constantly changes direction before settling down to a south-easterly, which is on the nose. It quickly reaches 18mph and our progress slows considerably. The plan had been to anchor off Nora, a Carthaginian city like Tharros only much larger. However, we shan't reach Nora at a reasonable time at this speed and David opts for Porto Malfatano instead. It turns out to be a good choice.

There are a number of anchorages here and we choose the one to the west of the Isla Teredda. It is an attractive spot and well protected from the wind. We anchor among an assortment of motor boats. Pottering between them are canoes and pedalos and the beach is dotted with tables, chairs and green umbrellas.

Being Sunday and a popular spot, there isn't really room for us. The bottom is also very weedy. It takes two attempts to get the anchor to bite and we are rather too close to the rocky island of Teredda in front of us. Pretty soon, however, the other boats begin to set off home for the night and we move into a nice big patch of sand in fifteen feet of translucent water.

A Hallberg Rassy flying a red ensign enters the bay. The English are famous for being antisocial to fellow countrymen abroad. Having arrived in a foreign paradise they are resentful at having another Englishman join them when they thought they had it all to themselves; or even worse, finding one already there. Accordingly, the middle-aged couple on the Hallberg Rassy, pukka in polo shirts and pressed shorts, stare steadfastly ahead as they pass our red ensign and anchor as far away from us as it is possible to get without beaching themselves. There may also be a fear of scratched topsides involved here, too, for this is a shiny, expensive new boat. They stand aloof and to our left. As the last day boat leaves, a Swedish sloop arrives and settles to our right, making just the three of us. And then an Italian Benetteau arrives.

I am frying fish sticks salvaged from melted ice; a bit soggy and not a particularly inviting color. David is trying for Monaco Radio's evening forecast. The mellifluous voice on Channel 68 has been absent from the VHF all day and when Channel 16 announces a gale warning about to be broadcast on another channel, although we re-tune to it immediately there is only silence. The Benetteau's cheerful young crew plunks its anchor beside the Hallberg Rassy's and settles alongside.

'Good grief,' I say, looking over at the middle-aged couple. 'They won't like that.'

They don't. They stand on deck in disbelief that the Benetteau could have anchored so close. The half dozen Italians aboard, blithely unaware, begin to party. The Monaco Radio forecast is for variable light-to-moderate breezes.

DURING THE NIGHT THE wind gusts up to 40mph, or Gale Force 8. It is a starry night and warm, but very dark and it is difficult to see where water ends and rock begins. The sea rushes from behind the island in front of us and crashes against the eastern face of the rocky cliff behind us. As the noise of water hitting rock gets louder with the increasing pressure of the wind there is the uncomfortable sensation that Voyager is edging closer to the rocks.

At dawn the Italian Benetteau dances away backwards toward the east cliff dragging its anchor behind it. After a struggle, several groggy revelers raise the anchor and leave the bay for another one next door to try for better holding. An hour later the Hallberg Rassy drags too. It is rather a shock. They had seemed too well-bred. They depart for the bay next door also.

After breakfast we are on our stern, hunched over the radio, with its aerial joined to a steel backstay for improved reception, listening to Monaco Radio. Its forecast for Sardinia is a fresh breeze from the south-west moderating in the evening, but we have difficulty hearing it because of the Force 8 roaring at us from the north-east. However, it's an ill wind that blows nobody any good and there's enough power going into our batteries via the wind generator to run the 'fridge off them for a while.

In northern climes wind strengths like these are invariably accompanied by cloud, cold and rain. Here it is hot, sunny and the sky is bright blue. People still come to the beach, although they tend to hold on to small children a bit more tightly than usual. It is also best to have nothing loose about you in the way of belongings or beach furniture. A traditional day on the beach is out of the question.

A couple with a young boy arrives first thing, carrying a large amount of luggage: umbrellas, chairs, food containers and a drinks-cooler. They stand for a while at an acute angle as they lean into the wind and then, with their luggage banging against their legs, set off back in the direction from which they have come. It is not the holiday they were expecting. The last to go is the boy, who looks wistfully at the water's edge and then trudges after them.

While it is an improvement on British cold, rain and cloud, it isn't the relaxed sailing we'd been hoping for either. The constant howl of the hot wind and the possibility of dragging are quite stressful, and one of us is always ready to sprint for the ignition keys the moment the anchor gives way.

Italy names the main winds after the direction from which they come. The one from the east is called the Levant. The Bora comes from the north and can blow from two to twelve days. There doesn't appear to be a name for the wind from the north east, but twelve days could put one helluva strain on the food cupboard. Still, the dark green sugar melon, currently in the cockpit and balanced on the rim of a bucket like the egg of some enormous mythical bird, should hold us for a day or two at least.

The wind rises steadily. Within an hour of the moderate forecast it is 47 mph and the beginning of a Strong Gale Force 9. On the beach, a large red-hulled sailing dinghy, beam-on to the wind, finally gives up the struggle and falls over onto its side. A family of four in swim suits settle down in its shade. Gradually, during the morning, the wind slackens to just below gale force and remains there. No-one leaves their yacht except at 1pm when a middle-aged couple in a red rubber dinghy hurtles out from the other bay and disappears behind our small island. A woman stands in its bow gripping the painter, Boudicca-style. Curious, I switch on our wind speed indicator. It is blowing 38mph.

It is still doing so at sunset when two yachts enter the bay. One is an elderly French Hirondelle catamaran with a failing exhaust, so that its engine goes *clatter-clatter clatter-clatter*. It clatters slowly down the anchorage and in due course passes behind us.

The other is a new Italian monohull. It has a vigorous man in his sixties at the helm, a sulky youth hunched in the cockpit and a young woman in a bikini on the bow. It roars down to the anchorage, bouncing violently on what is, after so much wind, a pretty rough sea. It halts beside the Swedish boat to our right and the helmsman begins a lively conversation with the startled couple in its cockpit. To hold a plunging 40-footer so close to another boat in such conditions without a collision takes skill. Or luck.

'By heck!' we say admiringly. 'There's style for you.' At the same time, given the increasing agitation of the Swedish couple, we are grateful that he hadn't been in a position to socialize with us.

Pleasantries over, he roars away to his chosen spot a short distance from the Swedish boat, which also happens to be the spot where we originally anchored on entering the bay and had trouble because of the amount of weed on the bottom.

Some years ago there was an advertisement on television which suggested playfully that Italian car drivers know only one speed—flat out—and that they drive as if they are descended from Roman charioteers. This must extend to boat owners, too, for this man appears to have modeled himself on Ben Hur.

Charging towards the shoreline, he bellows at the woman on the foredeck to drop the anchor. As he hasn't yet come to a stop, the boat naturally rides over the anchor and, since she hasn't had time to let out enough chain, the anchor fails to bite. Without waiting for the woman to retrieve the anchor, the helmsman goes into a violent turn. Unfortunately, because the anchor is still dragging along the seabed it restrains his bow and causes his stern to swing instead, sending it hurtling at high speed towards the beam of the Swedish yacht. The Swede and his wife stand in their cockpit watching it approach wide-eyed and with their knuckles between their teeth.

Against all the odds the young Italian woman retrieves their anchor—now encased in mud and shimmering weed—while the helmsman roars round in a circle and charges at the same spot again. Once there he repeats his earlier performance exactly and achieves exactly the same result.

The failure to get the anchor to bite can have only one cause and accordingly he leaves the helm and thunders forward to chastise the woman on the bow. She has just raised the anchor a second time—bearing even more mud and weed on it than before—and is bent double over the pulpit prising it off with a boat hook. He is too impatient to wait for her to finish doing this and orders it down again immediately. Then he goes bellowing back to his helm brandishing her boat hook above his head like a spear.

After this third attempt fails, the anchor emerges with several hundredweight of mud and weed clinging to it, which the woman is left to pick at ineffectually with her fingers since Ben Hur has carried off her boat hook. More roaring round in circles and bellowing follows.

At the fourth attempt the anchor finally bites, whereupon he storms up to the bow and, taking charge, lets out a further six feet of chain. Exultant, he stands on the foredeck, his feet wide apart and his fists on his hips in a gesture of triumph before returning to his cockpit.

THERE IS A SCIENCE to anchoring: a 3:1 ratio of anchor chain to water depth in mild conditions and a minimum of 5:1 in turbulent ones. *In extremis* Voyager's *capitano* has been known to hurl out 10:1 on the principle that it is safer to have out too much than too little. The Italian has dropped less than thirty feet of chain in fifteen feet of water. The Swede cups his hands around his mouth and pleads above the wind with the Italian to let out more chain. He is ignored and within minutes the Italian boat is dragging its anchor again.

Now apoplectic, the helmsman roars round in yet another circle and then hurtles off into the bay next door, bellowing. The youth still sits sullenly in the cockpit where he has remained throughout. The young woman crouches at the plunging bow contemplating the huge, green, glistening ball swinging violently from side to side in front of her, which is now the size of one of those things they use to demolish buildings. We, and the Swedes, sink back into our cockpit cushions emotionally drained.

Meanwhile, the French couple on the Hirondelle with the clatter-clatter engine have selected a sandy spot, lowered their anchor, let out plenty of chain, tested it to ensure the anchor has bitten, unpacked two small children and an elderly relative and have the kettle on by the time Ben Hur roars away.

Late evening I become aware of the sound of cicadas. The gale has passed over. The wind is falling away. Within an hour it is zero and the boats, instead of lying stretched out at the end of their chains are floating around their anchors like corks. There are a few desultory lightning flashes in the west, like a malign force retreating, but with luck we shall be able to set off for Sardinia's capital, Cagliari, tomorrow.

25

Malfatano to Cagliari

Next morning we wash our windscreen with the melted ice water and hurl buckets of seawater over the brown dust and salt encrusting our decks. The anchor is well buried and takes quite a bit of lifting. The plan is to anchor off Nora on the way, have lunch, and then go ashore to have a look around.

Shortly after leaving Malfatano we can see Capo Spartivento ahead of us. Our cruising guide says that a four-mile shoal stretches out from this cape, but our chart doesn't. David takes it wide to be on the safe side and confuses the hell out of four monohulls who have gone in close to shore. Once past the cape we make a left turn to follow the coastline again although despite our detour we are still just ahead of the four monohulls sailing close to the coast. A lack of wind means we are motoring and David increases our revs by a hundred to keep us ahead of their leader, a sloop with a red hull. What is it about men that always turns a convoy into a race?

'Why'd you do that?' I ask him.

'I'd'no,' he says.

Sometimes I wish David had chosen someone other than Homer Simpson as a role model.

We start to pull ahead. The red hull keeps pace with us, so its skipper has increased his revs, along with at least one of the others. A light tail wind springs up so David puts out our genoa which increases our lead. The man with the red hull puts out *his* genoa and increases *his* lead on the other boats. Genoas begin unfurling everywhere. They all have a similar problem with the tail wind, however. Like most monohulls when motoring, they already had their main sails up to stop them rolling. Now, with the wind directly on their sterns, their mains are shielding their genoas from the wind so that their newly-hoisted sails flap aimlessly. Within half an hour, all four are pointing out to sea, seeking a wind for all the sail they've put up and soon dwindle to four small white triangles in the distance.

Around noon, with tantalizing bits of Nora's ancient buildings in sight, Channel 16 announces a gale warning. Despite re-tuning to the working channels indicated, however, we can pick up no further information. The forecast gale might not arrive until tonight, tomorrow or could even be for an area so far away that the warning is irrelevant. Nevertheless, the wind has been rising steadily for some time and with the weather so unpredictable anyway we decide to leave Nora until another day and head directly for the shelter of Cagliari's large harbor instead.

SARDINIA'S CAPITAL LIES ON its south-east corner, at the top of a huge bay. It has two expensive marinas and a free public quay. We have no expectation whatever of finding a space vacant on the quay in mid-July. Amazingly, there are several.

As we approach we are spotted by Lyn and Toby to whom we'd chatted briefly in Carloforte marina over Toby's laundry. They sprint down the length of the quay towards us, drop their supermarket bags onto the hot concrete dock and reach out for our shore lines. I am very grateful. The top of the quay is above my head, and the only means of tying up to it is by threading your mooring ropes through the links of the enormously thick chain that runs across the top of it. The chain is too heavy to lift at arm's length, so I can't get a line under it. At the same time the links are too small to push a rope through one of them easily. With a strong offshore wind blowing, the result is that no sooner am I about to push the end of our rope through a rusty chain link than the wind blows the boat, me and my rope away from the quay again.

The best kind of yachtsmen embody the pass-it-on philosophy, that unconditional help one stranger extends to another for no other reason than that it is needed. There is no expectation of the good deed ever being repaid, as you will most likely never see each other again. It is an expression of do-as-you-would-be-done-by and when your turn comes, you will become that Good Samaritan who drops whatever you are doing, or leaves a warm, dry saloon in wind and rain to help someone get safely berthed.

Lyn and Toby express this spirit in spades. Not only do they abandon their food to the blistering heat to tie us up, they also scattergun essential information while they do it.

'There are no facilities,' pants Lyn, struggling to get our bow rope under the chain. 'But nobody bothers you, it's safe and it's free.' We will be grateful for this, as gale-force winds will extend our stay.

'The traffic's horrendous,' warns Toby tying up our stern. 'So do look out. But apparently if a car hits you on a pedestrian crossing, you get compensation.' His hands fully occupied, he inclines his head towards the west. 'The Tourist Information office is over there. The woman inside is very helpful and speaks very good English.'

26

Cagliari

Our priority next morning is to find somewhere to get our two propane bottles refilled. As Toby had said, Cagliari's traffic *is* horrendous, and unfortunately reaching anywhere from the quay requires crossing Via Roma, a nine-lane highway. At least, I think it is nine. When your thoughts are concentrated on your mortality it is always hard to be entirely accurate, but as far as I can work out—standing with our backs to the quay and looking out across it—there are two lanes going right, two going left, two right and three left. Two in the middle are for trolley buses and turn out to be especially disorientating. We stand on the kerb for a while and contemplate it all. There is no pedestrian crossing in sight.

Many years ago, on a visit to Rome, an habitué of that city instructed me on how to cross its infamous multi-lane highway. The key, he said, is to keep your nerve. Italian drivers will neither slow down nor stop, but once off the kerb neither must you. Maintain a steady and therefore predictable pace and the cars will go around you. Falter and you are done for.

My mother never visited Rome, which is fortunate because she was terrible at crossing roads. In that respect she had a lot in common with cats, which also hover uncertainly and then make a dash for the other side at the least appropriate moment. When that moment came, you needed to be in control of the situation because in her anxiety my mother would grip your elbow and, if you weren't alert, plunge off the kerb unwittingly thrusting you before her. The more anxious she got, the tighter her grip on your elbow.

Family and friends were so used to this habit that we were always prepared. But early in our marriage David took my mother into town for

105

the first, and what turned out to be the only, time. He returned ashen. As Ma headed blithely for the kitchen to put the kettle on he drew me aside. 'Your mother just tried to kill me,' he said. 'She grabbed me by the arm, and pushed me out in front of a 'bus.'

Over the years I have pondered this and other characteristics in relation to the nature versus nurture debate but have come to no conclusion. Whether through the genes or as a result of learned behavior I know not, but at moments of stress I revert to type. Gripping David firmly by the elbow now, I thrust him off the sidewalk and march him across nine lanes of traffic, including the two in the middle for trolley buses which, being unable to go around pedestrians, nearly prove fatal. On the far pavement he prizes himself free of my deadening grip.

'God!' he says, massaging life back into his elbow. 'You get more like your mother every day.'

THE WOMAN IN THE tourist office does indeed speak excellent English and is extremely helpful. She looks up *Gas Bottlers* in the local Yellow Pages and rings them for us but the plant only refills Italian bottles. With luck, she says, we should find somewhere to refill ours in Sicily.

We thank her for her efforts and accept a map of the town plus a booklet describing its historical treasures, available for viewing at minimal cost and with a brief history provided in English. The morning is already well advanced, however, so we decide to leave that for tomorrow, and head for the *supermercato* instead.

It is cramped and hot but the people it employs are quite extraordinary. In a narrow aisle, just me and a meat cabinet, I can't find the boned chicken I'm looking for. A manager materializes, from where I don't know, nor how he could have spotted me. Our communication consists of the Italian word for chicken, *pollo*, my mime, and his determination to provide what a customer wants—which he does.

Then there is the young woman on the checkout. She exhibits a trait we will notice throughout the town: the courtesy of ensuring that foreigners understand how much they have been charged followed by a quick review of their handful of change and the wrapped sweet.

27

A Walk Through History

U nless you're born to very high temperatures it is more pleasurable to get the bulk of any walking and climbing done early, and be on the home run by noon to a lazy lunch and siesta. Accordingly we leave Voyager before seven next morning and climb up to the old quarter known as The Castello. This is the ancient citadel, built on the high ground overlooking the port and the lagoons and it was once the seat of power. The sun is not up yet and the narrow cobbled streets are deserted and deliciously cool.

We pass the cathedral and the Torre di San Pancrazio, all still closed, and enter the grounds of the Arsenale for coffee. Once the site of the royal arsenal, it now houses the city's principal museums. They too are still closed, but its *al fresco* café opens early and is popular with men in overalls and industrial boots enjoying an espresso on their way to work. They are good-humored and helpful and pass the time of day with us as we sip our coffee.

From here we duck under, or walk around, the wizened little pine trees that dominate the sidewalks, then it's down the hill past the An-fiteatro Romano and the university, and into the Orto Botanico at the bottom. These botanical gardens are to be the furthest extent of our day's tour, and also its beginning. We arrive there just as it opens.

Its surprised but pleased attendant directs us to the café on the other side of the road to buy our entrance tickets. No bland pastel bits of paper these. Italy's *biglietto d' ingresso* are invariably little artistic gems, usually featuring some aspect of the site being visited. After clipping ours, and inviting us to sign his visitors' book, the attendant shoulders a fork and spade and dematerializes into the greenery. Some parts of the gardens are closed off to visitors for Millennium renovations but there is still more than enough left to captivate.

The gardens are cool, fragrant and shady in a morning already preparing to steam. I barely resist the urge to throw my arms around a long-stemmed water lily, at shoulder height on the edge of a raised pool, its enormous blossom luminous in a beam of sunlight. Everything here is enormous. We wander under soaring exotic trees, towering palms, house-sized yuccas and cacti that would dwarf the average bungalow—all the varieties familiar in small pots at home only this is their natural climate and here they can reach their full potential.

It is like shrinking to a fraction of one's normal size and tumbling down a rabbit-hole into Wonderland. The effect is heightened by the time of day and being the only people there. What little sun gets through is low and slants secretively through lush green foliage. Outside the high walls a hot, dusty city is just coming to busy life. Inside it is sensuous, magical.

To reach the Roman amphitheatre, the second stop on our itinerary, we have to climb back up the steep hill past the university. Its buildings are on both sides of the street, and you can guess at the disciplines without reading the signs. The political science department is flush with the sidewalk, its featureless wall spattered with black and white posters and its hovering students in dark clothes, bearded, solitary and tense. At the arts and social sciences faculties, across the road, flowers bloom behind a neat picket fence, piano music wafts from an open window and students in bright colors converse animatedly in groups.

Cagliari's 2nd century AD Roman amphitheatre originally seated around 20,000 people. It is visible from the street, and the animal pits and the corridors through which they were led onto the stage still exist. Dubiously eyeing the crane and scaffolding lying about the stage, we enter the iron gates. The attendant confirms our suspicions. The site is closed for millennium renovations. I read his name on his identity badge: Sandro, the male equivalent of mine.

He is deeply apologetic at being unable to allow us to enter the site, and so reluctant to turn away visitors disappointed that, apologizing profoundly for his considerable English, he invites us onto a platform overlooking the theatre and gives us a scholarly overview of its architecture and history. The Romans had put on scenes of sea battles here on real water. The seating had been cut from living rock. The site had once been vast, but most of it now lies buried under later developments and much of its stone was carried off to build churches in the Middle Ages. Even so, its acoustics are still so good that summer concerts are held here.

WE FIND THAT ONE museum or gallery per outing gives more pleasure than trying to take in too much; so back at the city's arsenal we choose the archaeological museum. It is small but beautifully laid out with a very helpful historical perspective. And after the pleasure of Tharros and the promise of Nora, it is an unmissable bonus to be able to go and see major Phoenician, Carthaginian and Roman finds representing aspects of everyday domestic life such as jewelry, coins, statues and one of my great pleasures, ceramic pots.

Most extraordinary of all, however, are the bronze statuettes from Sardinia's Nuraghic culture, which are also the main source of information about the mysterious people who built those three-and-a-half-thousand-year-old stone structures which still litter the landscape. Made as votive offerings, the little figures were buried in the ground which kept them out of the hands of raiders. Stylized and spindly, but evocative and surprisingly humorous, they show a wide range of life from nursing mother to warriors, hunters, shepherds and domestic and wild animals.

When we have completed our tour we are asked to fill in a questionnaire. The museum is eager to improve its accessibility and information. Everywhere you go in Cagliari, it seems, there is a desire to accommodate you.

It is there in abundance at Torre di St Pancrazio—St Pancras's Tower—part of the defenses the Pisans built after taking the city from the Genoans in 1305. We can't work out how you get into it, so I tap on the nearest door and ask. A cheerful man drops what he is doing and escorts us up six flights of an almost vertical wooden staircase. There isn't even an entrance fee. The view from the top, over the old town and the port, is superb. Going up is not bad at all, thanks to our altitude training at Mahon, but the staircase is open-fronted and as you descend its treacherously narrow treads there is nothing in front of you but sky.

We visit the cathedral and have a cold drink in Piazza Constitutione before buying fresh bread and little almond cakes in a side street. Then it is downhill all the way, back to the boat with them, to have with a lunch of tuna, smoked cheese and olives.

By mid-afternoon the temperature reaches 100°F and the decks are so hot you can't put a bare foot on them. Combined with a fierce hot wind, the effect is like living under a hair dryer on maximum heat. Despite a forecast for a moderate-to-strong breeze from the south-west, the wind reaches Gale Force 8 from the north-west and the sea is so choppy there are breaking waves inside the harbor.

The only variation in this hot, howling wind in several days is when it changes direction. Instead of blowing us all *off* the quay it now blows us against it, with such violence that the local chandler does a roaring trade in fat fenders as we rasp and scrape against the concrete quay. Nobody is going anywhere.

28

In Pursuit of Propane

One evening, during an amble round the old town, we decide to seek out some authentic Sardinian cooking for the following night. As well as saving on fuel, a meal out will also mean a really cold bottle of wine. To preserve what little propane we have left for cooking we are still turning off the 'fridge at night.

As we wander between restaurants, reading the menus on the windows, we notice a small lock-up shop with an assortment of propane bottles near the door. Stretching his English to the limit, the very helpful young man inside says he might be able to fill our bottle for us, but he would need to see it first. Could we bring it round tomorrow for him to have a look at? We smile at him wolfishly and ask what time he opens.

As we totter down the quay with it at 7.45 next morning a voice from one of the boats calls, 'Would you like to use the cart?' After days of sheltering from gale-force winds together there is a comradely, multi-national atmosphere among the yachtsmen lining the quay: Australian, Dutch, English, Danish, French, German, Austrian, American. We have shared information, advice, books, opinions and sugar melon; also a supermarket cart which has been rumbling back and forth along the quay since our arrival bearing water containers filled at the fish dock tap, diesel cans filled at the gas station on the main road, provisions from the supermarket and spare parts from the chandlers, all in preparation for the moment when the wind stops blowing to excess and we can all continue our journeys.

The cart is tempting because the gas bottle is large and heavy. Unfortunately the shop is reached via steep cobbled streets with narrow lumpy sidewalks so the only option is to carry it suspended between us using a piece of rope each as a handle. We get along fine as long as we keep in step. The only problem occurs while crossing the nine-lane Via Roma. It is the morning rush hour and quite awesome. We break our rhythm running out of the path of a trolley 'bus and the bottle takes on a momentum of its own. It sends us staggering drunkenly across two car lanes before we get it, and ourselves, back under control again.

We arrive at the young man's shop at the same time he does. He inspects the bottle and looks thoughtful. Yes, he says, he can fill it, but not until after the shop closes. What he will have to do is transfer gas from another bottle into ours and to do that he needs to be free of interruptions.

Joyously we thrust our empty bottle towards him and ask if he could possibly do a second one while he is about it. He agrees. However, there is another vital question to which we need an answer, before we stagger across the highway and up the hill a second time. Even empty, a large gas bottle is heavy. Filled with 28lbs of liquid gas it is deadly. Before presenting him with the second one we take the precaution of establishing that he is prepared to deliver. Tomorrow morning, he says, at nine o'clock.

By the time we have returned to Voyager for the second bottle, roped ourselves to it, made our assault on the Via Roma and climbed the hill to his shop, the morning is quite well advanced. When we get back down to the front again we are in need of refreshment and stop at one of the street cafés. It is not one we have ever stopped at before and the man serving is unknown to us. He puts the drinks on the table but before David has finished saying, 'Thank you,' the man growls, 'Pay me now!' We have no idea what it is about us that displeases him but it is the only time in the entire Mediterranean that we are asked to pay in advance.

MEANWHILE, WE HOPE THE young filler of gas bottles turns out to be as able as he is willing. We also hope he keeps his word regarding delivery since the wind has dropped and we should be able to leave tomorrow, although we shan't be heading for Greece as originally planned. In the light of the unseasonable and unpredictable nature of the weather we have decided to abandon our progress east. We are currently sheltering four days out of six because of gales or the threat of gales and in fourteen days on the Sardinian coast we have been able to travel on only five of them. The further east we continue, to Sicily and Malta let alone Greece, the more pressure we will end up putting on ourselves to get back to Gibraltar by late September in preparation for an Atlantic crossing.

When we worked full time and had only weekends and annual holidays in which to sail we sometimes ended up struggling through bad conditions because we had deadlines to meet back home. We don't have to do that any more, so it seems foolish to impose unnecessary stress or risk upon ourselves. Sicily, Malta, Greece, and even Turkey which we also long to cruise, will all still be there another year. In the meantime, The Balearic Islands are among the Mediterranean's most popular cruising grounds, yet we've seen relatively little of them beyond Mahon. We have therefore decided to have a leisurely poodle round the islands of Menorca, Mallorca, Ibiza and Formentera and then make our way comfortably to Gibraltar in time to make the most seasonable passage to Madeira.

That evening we sit over the menu in the small, modestly-priced restaurant we had identified the previous evening as serving Sardinian food. We choose what is described in the English translation as 'fish soup'. What arrives is a huge dish of hot shellfish in a thick tomato, onion and red pepper sauce, with neat wedges of coarse-textured bread thrust into the great pyramid of crabs, prawns and mussels. It is delicious, especially with our first bottle of wine in some time which is properly chilled. David even manages to spare the tablecloth.

NEXT MORNING AT NINE, a small three-wheeled van trundles onto the quay and our gas bottles are unloaded. A number of yachtsmen appear to congratulate us on finally getting them filled and remain to chat. The young man's bill must have taken him ages. It is carefully made out in English, explaining how much gas has gone into each bottle (the second one not having been quite empty) at how much per liter, down to the final item 'Transport Free'. David counts out endless lire notes into his hand.

When bottles like these are filled at a bottling plant the pressure is regulated and the weight of the liquid gas is carefully monitored to allow room for expansion in changing temperatures. With the method used by the young man this is not possible and they can over-fill. With the wind gone the morning is even hotter than ever and in the short time that the bottles stand on the quay, while the bill is explained and settled, the heat is enough to make the gas inside them expand. One of them begins to hiss and then a jet of highly explosive gas streams from its safety valve. The sunlight catches it and reveals a rainbow-colored fan of dancing molecules, like those trapped in a soap bubble, only moving much, much faster.

A moment before there had been a crowd of people on the quay. Now there is only David and the young man in sight. The latter takes a small spanner from his pocket and carefully reduces the pressure on the valve with the delicacy of a bomb-disposal expert. David watches what he does, then gingerly carries both bottles into the shade on our deck. *Use one for a day*, explains the young man before he leaves. *To reduce the pressure. Then use the other.*

David stows the bottles in the gas locker, connects one and we turn on the 'fridge. Then we make one last life-threatening dash across the Via Roma to the supermarket to restock it.

29

The Courtesy of Strangers

There are many places which are memorable for all sorts of reasons. Those you remember with the most affection seem to be the ones where the people make you feel good about being there simply by the way they treat you.

Cagliari is like that: the helpful staff in the tourist office and the supermarket; the workmen in the Arsenale coffee shop; Sandro bringing a Roman amphitheatre to life; the museum curator eager to improve accessibility for visitors; the young filler of gas bottles and the people in the streets who unstintingly gave us directions—sometimes offering assistance without even being asked, simply because they thought we looked lost. They have been kind, courteous, patient, helpful and scrupulous in their dealings with foreigners, yet in a quiet and unobtrusive way.

There was also the family that arrived on the quay at sunset the evening before we left. It was a Friday, and the end of what must have been a very hot working week even for Sardinians. They were a middle-aged couple, the woman rather bad on her feet, three young adults and a small boy. They smiled and nodded good evening as they passed, admired the boats—discreetly avoiding, as locals always did, your living quarters—and then two camping chairs creaked open.

At an appropriate distance from the boats, so as not to intrude on anyone's privacy, on a public quay their taxes would have paid for, the man settled his wife in one of the chairs and then seated himself in the other. The younger family members stood around them.

It was one of those glorious high-summer evenings when a massive sun, blazing like a foundry furnace, sets the whole sky on fire and turns the sea to molten gold. Wordlessly the family watched until it disappeared below the horizon. Then they folded the two chairs and went home as quietly as they had come.

30

Nora

....

After stowing the gas bottles and filling the refrigerator on Saturday morning we set off for Nora. We lunch on the way and anchor off the western side of the Capo di Pula peninsula three hours later. It is a strange experience. To our right is a beach packed with people: swimming, sunbathing, laughing, shouting, listening to radios and slapping on suntan oil. To our left are the ruins of a city begun by an ancient civilization more than 3,000 years ago.

In one sense the two scenes could have come from a Sci-Fi film, where the protagonist is caught in a tear in the time-space continuum. In another sense, the people on the beach are of course the missing element in places like Nora, where you tread carefully and even talk quietly, as if you are somewhere sacred. Whereas at one time even these revered of old stones once rang to the sound of people like those on the beach: shouting, laughing, slapping on oil, listening to music and generally enjoying themselves—only not if they were women of course. And given the Phoenician and Roman propensity for travel and colonization, including even Britain's chilly shores, their blood inevitably flows through the veins of quite a few of us who tread old stones like these; and for whom, could we but know it, this is as much a visit to the old family homestead as academic interest in an archaeological site.

David rows us ashore. Rising sea levels mean that the seaward perimeter of the city is under water, and we peer down over the sides of our dinghy at ancient paving stones. Founded, like Tharros, by the Phoenicians, settled by the Carthaginians and subsequently occupied and expanded by the Romans, Nora was abandoned around the third century AD.

Ashore we wander through its streets and the substantial remains of the amphitheatre with its mosaic floor, the ruined temple, shops, houses, warehouses and thermal baths, and wonder what living in the patrician house must have been like. And having lived during the late twentieth century in a village where the mains backed up every time there was heavy rain, I'm always impressed by the efficiency of Roman drainage. We are the only people there that afternoon and find it an atmospheric place, especially at its eastern shore, standing on a paved street and gazing out past tall pine trees and broken columns at the shining sea that is slowly claiming it.

By evening we are back at Malfatano, attached to the same patch of sand which saw us through a Force 9 gale. Only there is no roaring wind now, just the keening of a young seagull standing on a rock. It goes on for hours. Its mother watches over it discreetly, but refuses to feed it. It is time for the kid to support itself now.

Our own dinner is underway in the galley when there is a *phutt!* out in the cockpit. This is followed by a loud hissing noise and it is coming from the gas locker. The second gas bottle cannot wait a day to have its pressure reduced in the recommended manner and there are a few moments of frenzy as David applies a spanner to the pressure release valve and then changes over the connection so that we can start using it. After husbanding our propane supply for so long, we are now profligate with it—'fridge on high, hot baths, coffee and pancakes for supper—*anything* to reduce the pressure in the gas bottle.

31

Sardinia to Menorca

We need fuel and water for our return to Menorca and arrive at Carloforte's fish dock at lunch time. It is also Sunday. A couple from another boat help us tie up. As we untie and push their boat off for them, they tell us the fuel dock will open again at 3pm. We cook Sunday lunch and observe the arrival of a motorboat with two young men on deck. The one at the helm switches off the engine then both men step ashore and walk across to the kiosk to see what time it opens. Their boat begins to drift away. We attract their attention and they run back to it shouting instructions and two young women emerge from below and rush about looking for rope.

Neither the fuel dock, nor the service station behind it, opens so we settle down for the night. We dine on pasta with meatballs in tomato and basil sauce and gaze out across the bay, at low hills that are dissolving into soft curves of blue-grey and brown. As sunset approaches, small local boats return from a day's fishing or a family outing and there is much unloading of children, dogs and the day's catch.

Although the diesel pump opens at 7.30 next morning we don't get away until after ten. A local boat that we help to tie up gets served first. Then, after our fuel tank is filled the operator tells us he only accepts cash so we have to move the boat along the dock away from the pump while David trudges into town to find a bank. The first cash point rejects his card, the second displays a notice saying the machine is not on line. He walks between the two until one of them finally produces some money.

By the time he returns the supermarket along the quay is open so I get bread, milk and one of its tasty little pizzas each for lunch at sea. Unfortunately, in the meantime a super yacht has arrived filling up not only the pump area but all the rest of the dock as well, thereby wedging us in between itself and a newly-arrived boat belonging to the *Guardia Costierio*, the Coastguard. We wait for the super yacht to finish taking on its 2000 liters, but it still shows no sign of leaving as its skipper seems to have been sent off to get cash, too. He is gone a long time. We begin to think we shall never get away from Carloforte's fuel dock but finally the pump attendant and six coast guards take pity on us and lever us out.

The forecast is for south-easterly light-to-gentle breezes and a sea 'slight with ripples'. By 2pm it is virtually windless but with the sea heaving. Why it is heaving when there is hardly any wind we do not know, and can only assume it is the result of distant storms. A thunderstorm *is* forecast for later.

Since we are motoring and producing plenty of battery power I have decided to finish our latest newsletter. As the turbulence increases, however, sitting below and staring down at a computer screen produces the first stirrings of seasickness so I abandon the newsletter. Ultimately we pitch and roll, shimmy and fishtail and then rock so rapidly from side to side that all our bones get knocked just trying to sit still.

At least the wind rises a bit and is from behind, so we maintain a good speed. Eventually the sea calms down but it is still a strange evening, with a surface wind blowing in one direction, high cloud traveling in another and the sea running counter to both.

Heavy cloud obscures the setting sun until the last 10 minutes, but they are amazing minutes. Two strips of red cloud divide the blazing sun into three hot gold ingots. Slowly the cloud vaporizes into a ring, like Saturn's. When the sun reaches the horizon all the cloud disappears and for a few moments this vast red pulsating orb, with liquid gold inside it, hovers on top of the sea.

The impression of it actually resting on the water is so strong that I could swear there are waves bobbing behind it. Then it goes down, leaving me with a sense of abandonment, and vaguely apprehensive of the coming night. However, apart from a single echo on the radar screen, 11 miles to port, neither of us sees anything all night, least of all the forecast thunderstorm.

OUR LAST WATCH CHANGEOVER is at 7.45am and David has barely had time to settle into our bunk when I tiptoe down and whisper, 'You asleep yet?' over his closed eyes. We are always very tired at the end of our last watch and normally I would not have disturbed him. That's why I only whispered. Had he been asleep already, I should have left him to his rest. We see dolphins on a regular basis, after all, whereas the craving for sleep sometimes becomes all-consuming. But this morning some instinct sends me down to fetch him. And if I hadn't, he would never have believed what I told him when he got up.

They have come leaping from the north and we stand on the foredeck as eight of them put on a show. What *we* must look like from behind on these occasions, wearing various bits of night attire or sometimes only Factor 50+ and sunglasses, bottoms-up over the bow rail, only a distant tanker captain with powerful binoculars could tell us.

Individual dolphins of the same species are sometimes recognizable from one another by size, color or scars. Often, one will be larger than the others, have scars on its skin from fights, fishing nets or a boat's propeller, or appear to be the dominant member. Some of today's group look similar to those which performed for us on the way out—in particular, a large pale dolphin and a small dark one—and indeed we are back in the same vicinity. As soon as they get into their act we are sure it is them, only now they are better than ever. It is as if they had carried away the raw routines from their last visit to us, choreographed and rehearsed them, and returned with a polished performance.

As before, one dolphin swims inches in front of each bow, maintaining our boat's exact speed. Neither of them ever appears to glance at the pointed bit of hull a whisker from its tail. Two others fan sideways, above and below each other, backwards and forwards under each hull. This is a refinement of what they did before, and it is beautifully done. But they have also added something entirely new. In the space between our hulls, directly below us, the dolphin smaller and darker than the rest maintains a constant course under water, while the dolphin larger and paler than all the others does victory rolls over it. The large pale dolphin does this continuously while maintaining the same forward speed as its smaller partner and, with each roll, an eye meets ours to observe our reaction. It is a display of symmetry and production values worthy of Busby Berkeley and by now we are cheering and clapping.

When their performance ends, it does so with a proper finale. The six members of the chorus fan away under the hulls, one by one, until only star and partner remain. After one last roll they too glide away, one under each hull; first the straight man, and then the star—but only after one final, triumphant flourish.

We will encounter dolphins many more times, in many other places, but never do we see the like of this again.

The Balearic Islands

32

Menorca: Fornells

W e have a relaxed passage and a tasty lunch and arrive at Fornells at 6pm. It is always good to be anchored before dark and Fornells is the nearest safe harbor before we begin our tour of the Balearics. The harbor looks very beautiful in the early evening sunshine and instead of the little hamlet down the far end, we anchor off the village this time, it being handier for the pie shop next day.

We rise early, do our chores and go ashore. David rows us back with me balancing a warm tuna pie and apple slices for lunch. The day is quite still and the morning very pleasant but later it becomes hot. We do nothing in the afternoon as the heat and humidity become unbearable and the decks burn your feet. The coolest place on board is the sofa with all the windows open. This kind of excessive heat and humidity, about which even the local people complain, frequently precedes unsettled weather; and so it turns out.

We had been planning to leave tomorrow morning until we tune into Monaco Radio. The forecast is for near-gale-force winds from the northeast tonight and tomorrow and the bay David had planned to use for our first night's stopover is not a good place to anchor in a north-easterly wind, let alone one near gale force. It seems sensible to remain at Fornells and, for added protection, we move across the bay late morning to be nose-in to a small inlet that will give good protection from a strong nor'-easter. There is a Dutch boat, a Spanish boat and us, and between the three of us we fill the available space.

THE WIND RISES AROUND midnight, but comes from the north-*west*. We all swing round but are still well-protected. Half an hour later another yacht motors down our starboard side and begins anchoring virtually alongside the Spanish boat and directly in front of us. It is rude and dangerous. When the boat drags—as it must, since it is too close to us to let out sufficient chain—it will collide with our bows. On the other hand if the wind shifts, even a little, it will hit the Spanish boat.

However, we are soon in no position to observe what will happen, since in laying his own anchor the newcomer dislodges ours and we begin to drag quite quickly onto the inlet's rocky shore. There is a rush to switch on the engines and then raise our anchor in pitch darkness, a strong wind and a confined space. We are unable to re-anchor within the inlet as the position of the newcomer has ensured that there is now no room for us to do so safely.

Our only option is to leave and anchor elsewhere, although it is difficult to see where we are going. The sky is heavily overcast and the night so black that a torch seems to compound the darkness rather than illuminate it. We try another inlet a few hundred yards away but it is very crowded. The anchor doesn't bite immediately and we end up too close to the boat behind, its skipper flashing his torch at us to register his disapproval.

Out in the main harbor it is also packed, and we spend some time motoring around in heaving water looking for a place to drop our anchor. Fornells is a popular refuge in bad weather and the forecast has brought in boats from all-over looking for shelter. We decide to try the area near the village that we had left late yesterday morning. As we cross the harbor in the darkness there is a terrible howl as wind and water roar in through the heads.

Gales are enormously stressful. It's not just fear of damaging your boat or somebody else's, although obviously that is part of it. It's the *noise*. It scrapes at your nerve-ends. It drives you mad. The wind howls. The sea booms. Waves bang against your beam and up under your bridge deck. Water sucks and snorts in the cockpit drain-holes, rushing up when you least expect it, making you jump and soaking your feet. The wind whines relentlessly through your rigging on a single, unwavering note until you feel you would do almost anything to make it stop. At the same time, all the boat's normal, easy rhythms vanish. Instead, you lurch and bounce so that at the very time you need to move quickly, all you can do is drag yourself slowly from handhold to handhold. Everywhere is ceaseless noise and erratic motion, as if every part of your boat is under assault. It is at its worst when you are unable to see what is happening around you, when you are enveloped in pitch darkness.

When we arrive off the village it is not only very crowded but boats are dragging everywhere, torches are flashing and people are shouting at one another. Trying to find somewhere in this chaos is futile. Nor is finding a suitable spot elsewhere helped by the fact that a number of boats have no anchor lights showing. An anchor light is a legal requirement, but cruisers sometimes ignore the need for one in order to save battery power. So you get to what looks like an empty space only to find boats in it.

The plan then is to try anchoring off the little hamlet down at the bottom of the bay where we had anchored during our previous visit; although inevitably that anchorage will be full, too. We are only half way there when we find that we are already in calmer water, well away from other boats and in a suitable depth for anchoring, so we decide to try our luck here.

It is roughly half way between the harbor's western shore and the larger of the two small islands off the eastern shore. This larger island has two light houses on it which act as leading lights for boats entering the harbor at night. It is an exposed position in a direct line with the harbor entrance and the opposite of everything David had tried to achieve in the way of protection for us by anchoring in the small inlet, but our anchor bites and holds superbly. Even so, with all the dragging going on around us we maintain an anchor watch and take turns sleeping. There is always an adrenaline rush until you get the boat to safety. Then tiredness overwhelms you.

At least our watches are not boring. There is something constantly going on, accompanied by blazing torch beams, bobbing anchor lights and bad language as someone sees off an intruder and the outcast reluctantly seeks another place to drop his anchor. Gradually the sky lightens with the approach of dawn.

It is a bad night, however, and most boats have to re-anchor at least once; some of them often. One poor man, a Scandinavian in an aluminum boat, has his anchor drag at least eight times. By morning he looks demoralized and very tired. The wind reaches 37mph during the night and continues into the following day although it is quite pleasant sitting out in a sheltered cockpit. You can't go ashore, of course. Wind and waves continue to roar into the bay, and in the daylight you can see that the waves are hitting the headland either side of the entrance with such force that sea spray is flying right over the top of the cliffs.

We are a long way from the village. To try reaching it across the rollers crashing in through the heads in a small dinghy with a very small outboard engine would be madness, and we need to stay aboard anyway in case Voyager drags. So while David upends himself into the port engine bay to find out why there is a small but persistent leak of sea water into it, I sit outdoors and finish our latest newsletter home. Our position gives an uninterrupted view up and down the whole harbor and there is much to observe.

In the Bad Seamanship Stakes there is a tie between a French 36-foot cutter-rigged sloop and a similar-sized Austrian motor yacht which both drag their anchors up the length of the harbor through dozens of anchored boats for hours. They frequently come close to colliding with other boats, and constantly risk dragging up other people's anchors with their own, not least the exhausted Scandinavian in the aluminum boat. They know they are dragging but do nothing about it. Periodically they emerge on deck, look around, yawn, scratch and go below again. The skipper of the motor yacht even comes on deck with a video camera as he travels slowly backwards up the harbor. Unable to believe he can know he is dragging and do nothing about it I yell to him and signal his situation, but he simply films me waving and goes below again.

Meanwhile the sailing dinghies come out. Despite a couple of superb maneuvers, however, in a 35mph wind it is effectively a mass capsize drill. They go down like nine pins, hauling themselves upright only to capsize again almost immediately. The two RIBs containing the instructors, which hurtle between them, spend much of their time above the water as they hit wave after wave at speed. Neither gets so spectacularly airborne, however, as a sailboarder just before he lands face first with an appalling crash.

After about six hours and a distance of three-quarters of a mile, the owner of the dragging sloop finally pulls up his anchor and re-sets it. The motor yacht continues a further four hours and covers about one and a quarter miles before dragging to a stop at the far end of the bay. At the same time I can hardly believe how firmly we have sat out these testing conditions. Since settling alongside the island, Voyager has been rock solid. Can the English anchor, or *what?*

ON SATURDAY MORNING THE wind drops, which is convenient as we run out of water washing up the breakfast things. We dinghy to the village to shop, post a birthday card and fill plastic containers with 28 liters of water at the public fountain. We also discover that it is Fiesta. The little village square is already stripped for action. There is sawdust covering the road for the horses and wooden stands have been put up around its sides.

Menorca's fiestas are colorful, traditional affairs of parades of civic worthies, children, religious ceremonies and immaculately-attired riders on glistening horses which on command will rear up and prance on their hind legs. The horses are richly ornamented and their manes plaited, and there are usually quite a lot of them in a confined space full of people yelling, blowing whistles and strident brass horns and thrusting an arm at them to make them rear up onto their hind legs. A sort of horse's Hell, really. This part is very popular. Its genesis, like that of the fiesta itself, is thought to originate in the Middle Ages. Its purpose seems to be to show what stupendous control the rider has in keeping a highly-strung animal up on its hind legs long enough for the drunken reveler lying under its front hooves to be dragged to safety by his friends.

We take our shopping and water back to the boat and return in the evening. By then, the pie shop window has been converted to a Jug and Bottle, and one of the wooden stands is occupied by the most vibrant, irresistible band we have ever heard. Its Latin rhythms are conducted by a young dynamo using a whistle and a smoking fog horn, and even set David shimmying, which takes a lot. The younger and more adventurous dance fully clothed into the sea.

Observing people in a confined space repeatedly goading excitable stallions to rear up in front of them, you wonder if it might have been a form of medieval population control. Another possible form takes place after the band departs, when adolescents dive headfirst off the wooden stand and expect somebody on the ground to catch them. The ambulance sirens are still going at 4am.

Before leaving the boat I'd smoked the last of my cigarettes. I'd tried to buy more in the village but none of the bars appeared to sell them. The barmen had looked irritated and one actually waved me away, as if I was trying to scrounge a smoke, not buy some. I didn't mind. There are times in every addiction when, notwithstanding some painful effort on your part, escape is possible. Being distanced from its source helps and I returned to the boat empty-handed.

When David hauls up the anchor next morning we discover why we have sat out gale-force winds so firmly. The anchor is very difficult to lift and, after a lot of heaving and straining, it finally breaks the surface with a thick black cable tangled in it. We have spent the last two days hooked onto the electricity cable (not marked on our charts) supplying the island's two lighthouses.

WE HAVE A WINDLESS motor from Fornells, along Menorca's north coast. We are low on fuel as well as out of water so we head for Cuitadella's fuel dock. It is Sunday and we arrive at lunchtime, too late to catch the fuel dock before it closed for the day at 1pm. We go and anchor nearby until it opens again on Monday morning. Despite the fact that arriving places at lunchtime has been a feature of life with David, this particular occasion enrages me. I am *furious*. My fury is out of all proportion to anything short of a major act of betrayal. It is more appropriate to soap opera: a character's discovery of a partner's adultery with a best friend, for instance, or arriving home to find the house trashed by a teenager's party. David stares at me horrified. I am in my first day of nicotine withdrawal.

Next morning when we return to the fuel dock we discover that it doesn't do water. This makes me extremely irritable and I tell David that I'm not going to be able to cope with this sort of life after all. Getting the basics takes all your time, I complain. And there's the heat. I had been looking forward to a bit of dry warmth, I grumble, not being cooked alive. I perspire all the time. And my hair is going moldy. I've had enough, I say. *Enough!* I want to go *home*, only you've bloody *sold* it! My head is throbbing and my whole body aches. This is Day Two of nicotine withdrawal.

33

Mallorca: Bonaire

Once we have left Cuitadella's sheltered harbor we can see our next destination: Mallorca. Our first stop there is Puerto de Bonaire in a stunningly beautiful bay surrounded by mountain ranges and forests running down to the sea. To be truthful, we'd have come here even if it had been surrounded by spoil tips because the cruising guide says Bonaire's marina has two washing machines.

When I had bemoaned the dearth of launderettes in Spain to a friend at home during the winter, she had looked aghast. 'I thought you'd spend your time naked like Rosie Swales,' she'd said, her illusion of our unfettered life at sea severely impaired. Unfortunately, one tends to draw a bit of a crowd trawling the cheese counter at the local Spar in the buff. And even the most modestly-priced restaurant has a minimum dress code. There is also sunburn to contend with.

It really does grow, laundry. Add to basic clothing the boat's entire stock of towels and bedding and full bin liners start to encroach on your living space. And we *have* let it go a bit. In fact, another week and we really shall have to go native. It is all sorted ready and bagged, however. All it needs is the appropriate sound effects—the soft *click* of a little round glass door closing, and the *clunk* of a coin dropping into a metal box.

WE ARRIVE AT BONAIRE marina around 6pm. It is an attractive place, but the high concrete sea wall behind which it shelters seems to have absorbed the day's heat and be hurling it back out again. It is *hot*.

'How many nights do you want to stay?' the manager asks.

'Are the washing machines working?'

'Yes,' he says.

'Three nights, then.'

'You have a lot of laundry?'

'Yes. Could we have the key now, please?'

The manager is a heavy-set man with jet black hair and a thick moustache. He wears official-looking khaki and has large, dark mournful eyes that suggest they have seen everything life has to offer. His heavy black eyebrows lift slightly. 'All night?' he says.

'No,' I say, 'but I'd like to start at dawn and you won't be here then.' He continues to stare up at me from his chair and I add by way of encouragement, 'The heat's getting to me.'

'The heat's getting to all of us,' he corrects somberly, his eyelids drooping with exhaustion. But he hands me the key.

The little room containing the two precious machines is at one extreme of the marina, and our boat is at the other, so next morning my bicycle is invaluable. Unfortunately, heavy bags on both handlebars acquire a momentum of their own. Swinging haphazardly, they cause the front wheel to follow suit and I zigzag drunkenly back and forth across the marina. At one stage I narrowly avoid hurtling down the boat-lifting ramp and into the harbor.

David, meanwhile, is using his bicycle to scour the chandleries of the neighboring town. At Fornells he had finally traced the seawater leak in our port engine bay to a hole in the silencer on the engine's exhaust, which discharges diesel fumes and the water used to cool the engine. Now he is trying to find a replacement exhaust box.

I do seven washing machine loads. It takes from 7am until 3pm because they are elderly machines, small and very slow. Over an hour is also wasted when the one on the right refuses to open after its first load is finished and I have to wait until a marina attendant arrives for work at nine. Wordlessly he goes into a shed, emerges with a screwdriver, follows me into the laundry, rams the screwdriver in between the machine's door and its rim, levers the door open and departs. On my next trip I take along my own screwdriver.

And then it rains. This is the first rain we have seen in seven weeks. It is also the first time in two and a half months that I have had access to a washing machine. The rain is torrential and brings down with it all the airborne soil that the wind has carried up into the atmosphere over many weeks from all those arid, red-brown hills, so that when the rain lands it is red-brown too. I just keep going. The rain will stop sometime but tomorrow the machines might be out of order, the electricity might fail, or Annie from Humberside—the scourge of Alicante marina's launderette—might arrive with a dozen bags. The rain does stop after 24 hours, although damp washing kept in plastic bin liners, even for a day, smells horrible. Once out of its bags there is so much of it that there is barely room to hang it all out in one go, even using the outhauls as well as all the rails *and* slinging washing lines between the fore and back stays. Voyager looks like a slum tenement.

The log for the following day contains just one word: *Ironed.*

I don't mind. I need to keep busy. And with electricity and unlimited water available, after ironing everything in sight short of the sails, I throw myself into boat-cleaning, vacuuming and polishing. After the hyperactivity comes a day of exhaustion so total I barely leave my bed.

WHEN WE HAD APPROACHED Bonaire marina we had tied up on the reception dock at the entrance while we waited for a place to be found for us. However, we were told to stay where we were as there was no space available on the pontoons. There wasn't much room on the reception dock either, as most of it was taken up by a very large, new and expensive motor yacht, with a large new dinghy and a new and expensive jet ski tied to it. There hadn't been room to pull onto the dock without damaging the jet ski, which was a bit of a temptation but I thought better of it, and as there was a pair of legs hanging over the stern I called out the name of the yacht. The legs over the stern were pulled in and a large German lumbered upright, moved the jet ski, tied us up and then prostrated himself again.

Within a short time five much younger Germans returned to the brand new motor yacht from a jaunt ashore. A trap door in its hull opened and a brand new quad bike emerged and they trooped off down the quay with that. We spent the next three nights in close proximity to them as our boats were very close, stern to stern, and their cockpit loomed over ours.

They seemed to be on a business bonding trip and after their evening meal sat on their afterdeck, directly over our bed, talking and playing music—Edith Piaff and The Mamas and The Papas—until 3am and never breakfasted before eleven; whilst we'd been working since seven, quietly so as not to wake them, because in every other respect they were considerate, whimsical, oddly affectionate and despite being German never once took off their clothes in public.

Apart from their skipper, who may also have been their boss, they knew nothing about boats and approached each new task in a polite, curious group, the way very young children do, or very bright people taken from their natural orbit and without enough to occupy their usually busy minds.

Although they spoke English, we didn't converse as such. We saved their jet ski (God help us) from damage under the concrete dock when their boss was out and they forgot to tie it up properly; they rushed for their boathook when our bucket fell overboard. We took their lines and tied them back up when they returned from a sail and they all stood along their rail in a line blinking amiably at us the way people unacquainted with boating always do; until their boss shouted at them for not hopping ashore and tying the boat up themselves instead of keeping us out in the rain, and they all clambered over the rail together in a heap.

We emerged into our cockpit on one occasion as they were hosing down their afterdeck. They looked down at us and winced. 'Are we splashing you?' enquired one anxiously. We emerged again later to see three of them directly above us solemnly waving a blue and gold European Union flag on a pole, probably to dry it. I don't know why I did it: partly, perhaps, because they looked so comically serious that I decided to interpret their flag-waving as a challenge; and partly because for me the large EU flag currently wafting over my head, with its circle of little gold stars on its insipid blue background represented the increasing assault on Europe's great variety of national identities and cultures by a relentless central bureaucracy.

Whatever the reason, I went below for our red ensign, stood in the cockpit and waived it aloft in a cross between a football match and Last Night at the Proms and sang, 'There'll always be an England' to them. Unfortunately for my grand gesture I only know the first two lines of this rhyming jingoism, so after exhausting them and la-la-ing the rest of the verse, I folded my flag, gave a low bow, and went below again—to loud applause.

If their being there *was* a bonding session it was an unqualified success. Had they burnt joss sticks and ohmed, or smoked enough pot to envelop our boat as well as their own, there could not have been a greater sense of harmony on that cramped reception dock.

Or maybe it is all my own state of mind, for I *am* feeling indescribably happy. Euphoric, in fact.

THE WEATHER MEANWHILE HAS become settled and quiet. We have no need to look for protected anchorages at present and after leaving Bonaire are able to loiter in a number of beautiful bays. At San Vicente we lie between two extremes of leisure craft. Just off the beach there are little pedalos, with a chute on the front for children to slide down into the water while their parents pedal. While at the bay's entrance the Marie Cha III rides at anchor, 147 feet long and holder of the transatlantic record for sailing vessels, having crossed from New York to England in something like three and a half days.

When her RIB passes us on its way back from shore-leave its young skipper smiles and salutes us and I am touched to the heart by his gesture. When David puts on a 1960s compilation tape and the late Karen Carpenter sings the opening bars of 'We've only just begun to live,' I begin to weep for her. This is my sixth day without nicotine. So far I have passed through rage, irritability, hyperactivity, exhaustion and euphoria. I have now entered the maudlin stage.

34

Mallorca: Sóller

O ur next destination is Sóller but on the way we stop for lunch at Cala de la Calobra. It is a beautiful bay with a dramatic split in its high cliff face through which a water course called Torrente de Pareis flows down from the mountains and joins the sea. It is not even a trickle at the end of July, let alone a torrent, and people are sunbathing on its pebbles; so many of them in fact—sitting shoulder to shoulder and looking resentful—that there is barely room for us to land our dinghy. When a tourist coach or ferry takes you somewhere, you have sometimes seen and done all you want, or are too hot and tired to do more, long before you are collected again. One of the privileges of private transport is that when you have had enough you can leave.

From the small pebble beach you walk through the great cleft in the rock into a lagoon, although it is green sludge today. Even so, the geology of the place, and indeed the whole coastline, can only be described as spectacular, with stunning rock formations among towering cliffs.

As we resume our journey to Sóller something seems to happen to the light. As I stand on our stern and look back, harsh brown rock has softened into muted shades of blue-green and its ragged edges have melted into curves. I take three photographs. When the prints come back from the developer all the other images have normal colors and sharp outlines, but these three are ethereal. They are monochrome, the color of jade, and harsh peaks have become sinuous lines.

THE PORT OF SÓLLER is in a huge circular bay surrounded by mountains, its dogleg entrance making it very sheltered. You enter this stunning harbor between two lighthouses while ahead of you is a beguiling waterfront of village shops with wooded hills behind and the mountains beyond. As we anchor around 5pm, the first distinctive sound we hear is *Poop!* from an Edwardian tram sparking its way across the front. It is brown and orange, with three open-sided carriages, and it runs two miles uphill from the port's delightfully old-fashioned village to the old rural town of Sóller, which was built well inland from the port as a defense against pirates. We take a trip there next day.

The two-mile tram journey takes 20 minutes, through orange and lemon groves, smallholdings and allotments; alongside dry river beds; past people's patios with terracotta pots of Busy Lizzy, wrought iron chairs and tables and green wooden window shutters; gardens of dahlias and roses; runner beans; lime trees and bamboo.

Where it *poops* its way into the old town of Sóller it reduces the sidewalk to little more than a couple of feet. Then it cuts straight through the town centre and up to the narrow-gauge railway which runs between Sóller and Palma and the small station that houses its Victorian electric train.

Just before it reaches this railway station the tram rattles through the middle of the big leafy square that dominates the town's centre. It slices between the chairs and tables of the cafes under the trees, and it is a matter of fine judgment—at those tables nearest its rails—as to when and how far you extend your elbow when raising your coffee cup to your lips.

TODAY IS OUR 35ᵀᴴ wedding anniversary. We still exchange cards, but stopped buying each other presents some years ago except those things which can be eaten, drunk or arranged in a vase. To have bought each other non-consumables just meant something else to put in store or give away. Instead, we would have an outing to somewhere we had always intended to go, do some chore the other disliked doing for a month, or try to change a habit. This year I have given David something for which he has never asked, but which I know he has wanted for a long time because he wants us to spend a healthy, active old age together. I once read somewhere that nicotine can be as hard to give up as cocaine. I don't know if this is true or not, but if it is I have gone cold turkey and, though still a bit unstable, my gift to him this year is that I have become a non-smoker.

We celebrate our anniversary by taking the Edwardian tram into Sóller and then the Victorian train to Palma. There is a slight delay in the train's departure as our carriage has broken a spring and a large group of stocky men in blue work clothes and industrial gloves descend on it. Some become lost from view underneath it while the rest form a watching arc around the spot where they disappeared. The carriage interior is dark mahogany with brass fittings and the kind of reversible seats remembered from the trams and trolley buses of childhood, where the back of the seat swings on sturdy iron hinges depending on whether you prefer to travel with your back to the engine or not.

The journey to Palma takes an hour and crosses the Tramutana mountain range: past terraced hillsides, checker board olive groves, secluded farm houses and tidy fields with short-legged chairs under shady trees. A few miles out from Sóller the line curves around the hillside and you look back down onto the old town that you so recently left, cradled by the mountains, its stone buildings glowing gold in the sunshine. The name Sóller comes from the Arabic word *Sulliar* meaning golden valley.

Now and again the train clatters into tunnels. They are short and airy and almost immediately you smack out again into bright sunshine, except for one long one which causes the carriage's ornate ceiling lights to come on and sends a strong smell of mold from the tunnel walls rushing in through the open windows.

It is a delightful journey. At one end of the line a sleepy rural town, and at the other a bustling city, for despite its narrow streets and shady squares that is just what Palma is. We collect our mail from the *poste restante* section of Palma's vast marble hall of a post office, get five rolls of photographic film developed at ruinous cost and have a celebratory lunch.

35

Mallorca: Andraitx

Our next stop is Andraitx, which somehow we only ever seem able to pronounce as Anthrax, but that may have something to do with our feelings about the poisonous nature of its fishing fleet. We try three times to set an anchor outside the harbor but it won't bite into the rocky bottom. So we go onto the public quay. A group of Spaniards tie us up, and then we do the same for a Dutch family.

There are no lazy lines at Andraitx so you have to use a kedge anchor to hold your boat off the quay. We haven't done this maneuver since the charter sailing holiday in Yugoslavia nine years ago which started all this, and never with Voyager. It involves dropping an anchor off the stern several boat lengths before your bows reach the quay, tying up the bows and then hauling on your stern anchor rope until your bows are close enough to the quay to allow you to get on and off but not close enough to make contact with concrete. And you really need three people to do it without stress. It seems a nice little place with a splendid supermarket and we have fresh salmon for dinner.

Our kedge anchor comes adrift sometime after 3am and we are woken by our starboard bow nudging the quay. We get up and I pull the anchor in while David lowers the dinghy. I lift the anchor into the dinghy and David rows two boat lengths out and drops the anchor again. By the time he has returned, made sure the anchor is set, ensured that we were well off the quay, and pulled up the dinghy it is 4am. We are about to return to bed when the town's 15-strong fishing fleet—trawler-size—roars out causing a wash you would not *believe*. Standing on deck looking down the row of yachts along the quay it is like watching giant piano keys during a particularly frenetic piece of music. The boats plunge and crash. The kedge anchor of one of them is pulled up and its pulpit hits the concrete dock on a downward plunge with such violence that even four boats along it makes your teeth rattle. Had David still been in our small aluminum dinghy at this moment, re-laying our own kedge anchor, I could probably have said goodbye to *him,* never mind our bows. We decide not to stay a second night.

After a longish period at anchor, however, we are now on our second tank of water, so before we leave we walk over to the marina to see about buying some. As we approach the pontoons a number of yachtsmen are returning from the supermarket carrying large quantities of bottled water, which is never a good sign. We ask them about the stuff that comes out of the taps here and they say to forget about it. Our next destination is Ibiza but the cruising guide warns about water quality there, too, so we decide to stop off at Palma for some.

36

Mallorca: Palma

It is a windless journey to Palma in a calm sea. The only things stirring are very large, expensive motor yachts. As well as being the last word in luxury, they also have massive engines. They are designed for speed and their speed creates a massive wash.

The fundamental difference between those who own motor yachts and those who own sailing yachts is training. You cannot simply climb onto a sailing yacht and expect to sail it. In particular, there is a skill to setting canvas in relation to wind direction and strength that has to be learned. And while you learn how to handle the boat, you will also be taught the rules of the road and your responsibilities towards other craft.

Those who buy motor yachts often don't feel the need to take any lessons as the controls of a motor yacht are not unlike those of a car. They can simply step aboard, switch on the ignition, take the wheel and open the throttle. Before driving their car, however, they needed a license for which they had to pass a test, which included knowing which side of the road they were supposed to be driving on. Too often motor yacht and motor boat owners do not appear to know on which side of a channel they are supposed to pass another vessel, or that they are required to give way to certain types of craft under certain conditions. Their worst offences, however, relate to speed.

Some of the blame must lie with some of the manufacturers. They market their boats on their speed and the impressive amount of wash they leave in their wake, and the hulls are shaped to provide both, regardless of the damage they do in terms of other boat owners or the erosion of waterfronts and river banks. On top of this, at slow or even moderate speeds some power boats handle so badly that they embarrass their drivers. The result is that they roar from A to B in a straight line as fast as possible while being entirely indifferent to, or even immensely proud of, the wash they create. They are at their worst when they travel in packs, and when two or more of them roar down either side of slower, smaller or lighter vessels it can sometimes be a matter of survival for those left in their wake.

The earlier part of our journey to Palma is blighted by power boats. Despite weighing 11 tons Voyager is not immune from their wash and is bounced like a cork in a barrel when two boats, traveling in tandem, roar down either side of us. David instinctively rises to rescue a coffee mug and is thrown backwards against the arm of the helmsman's chair, scraping off a layer of skin all down his upper spine.

Happily the boats disappear at lunch time and apart from us little moves. The August afternoon is hot and windless and the few people in the small leisure boats we pass are languid and lazy. It is an afternoon to simply drift, and those we pass are doing just that. One small yacht is wallowing with its sail up, but it can only be for the shade. Another yachtsman is in the water cooling off, while his dog sits patiently in their dinghy, watching him. People lie on their backs in day boats under umbrellas with their feet hanging over the sides, and small children dangle fishing lines. We already have all the hatches open but it is so hot in the cockpit we open the two front windows to create an artificial breeze. It is very pleasant.

We have just entered the Bay of Palma when, out of nowhere, a very large new motor yacht roars straight at us, its black fenders bouncing along its gleaming white sides. Its speed alone would have been bad enough, but it passes so close to us that we catch its wash at its very worst. As David grips the wheel to steady Voyager against the onslaught I see the man on the motor yacht's flying bridge turn his head briefly to look down at us with vague indifference as he passes. But by then the realization of what he has done has sent me running for the saloon to slam down hatches and grab towels and try and minimize the damage as much as I can.

The wash hits us with such tremendous force that it rises eight feet high—the biggest we have ever experienced—and sends seawater pouring in through the open bow windows and ceiling hatches into the saloon. It soaks the sofa, carpet, the coffee table, books, charts, audio tapes and the hugely expensive photographs we had had developed in Palma. Worst of all, our costly radio with its SSB facility that provides weather forecasts on shortwave and will be our only source of information during an Atlantic crossing, has caught the full force of the water.

It is only later, when I have mopped and raged, that I remember the people lolling in their small boats, the children fishing, and the dog in the dinghy, because after the power boat had shattered our afternoon with its monstrous wash it had been heading straight for them.

I vow that I will never sail to Palma again. We have done so twice now, and both times have ended up mopping out the saloon, although the damage inflicted by a gale-force hailstorm is as nothing compared to what a selfish man on a powerful motor yacht can do. Nor do I ever want to enter the Réal Club Náutico marina again. We have been twice now and both times refused water, the first time even though we had already paid for it. Today we tie up on its visitors' dock for the second time. It is a long marina and its office is at the extreme end of it. It is the hottest part of a very hot afternoon as David sets off on the long walk to ask for a berth. We have two priorities: to get our expensive radio seen to as fast as possible before the seawater ruins it; and to wash our saloon furnishings. The office is closed for lunch until 4pm.

We had noticed on the way into the marina that there were spaces available on the public dock, but our cruising guide says there are no facilities there. Since we are afraid to use what water we have remaining in our tank for cleaning until we are sure of its replacement, we wait until four o'clock and then David walks between the long rows of wall-to-wall luxury motor yachts to the office again. We cannot have a berth, the receptionist tells him, without a reservation.

David explains our situation and asks if the marina will sell us water before we leave so that we can clean up the damage caused by the motor yacht. We cannot have water, she tells him, without a berth.

He returns from another long walk in the intense heat and approaches the fuel dock which is just opening. Although it sold water last year, this year it doesn't. A French yachtsman, overhearing, very kindly comes across to tell us that water has recently become available on the public quay from 9-1pm daily. We leave the marina and tie up at the public quay and spend that evening and the following day washing, rinsing, and drying.

The problem with seawater is that it never dries out; the salt continually absorbs moisture from the air so that everything remains clammy and ultimately becomes moldy. It also rots upholstery foam and carpet backing. I use all the water we still have on board and we fill and refill our tanks next morning before the water gets turned off at 1pm. The man who comes for the overnight fee, plus a small charge for water, speaks no English but observes the entire movable contents of our saloon laid out in the sun on every available inch of deck. He takes no deposit for the water fitting and indicates wordlessly where we can leave it if we go before he returns at 1pm to turn off the water, thereby saving us walking to his office with it. We know his office is miles away, on the other side of the harbor, and we think him very kind.

Most of the sofa's fourteen upholstered cushions have been either splashed or saturated, the loose cushions are drenched. All the towels that were washed at Bonaire have been used to mop up books, tapes and radio. To make matters worse, copies of our 8-page newsletter had been printed off. The ink has dissolved in the seawater and contributed to the mess. Nor will we be able to recover our losses, since marine insurance carries a large excess. There would also be our no-claims bonus to lose.

I can at least work in the shade. David's priority is our radio so he spends his time in unrelenting heat rushing between people who are said to know where there is a specialist in repairing radios, who turns out not to be when he gets there, but who knows somebody who is—and always at opposite ends of the town. When he finally finds the specialist his verdict on our radio is, 'Kaput,' and David begins another search, this time to find a replacement.

His search ends at Palma's premier department store, El Corte Inglés. Ever the provider, and aware of the absence of food shops near the boat, he also goes around the store's food hall. Unfortunately, El Corte Inglés only sells fruit and vegetables in sealed packs. So along with a new radio, chicken, some divine cake and fresh (filleted!) sardines for dinner he returns with 8 lemons, 9 heads of garlic, 10 kiwi fruit and an armful of leeks.

Not surprisingly he is weary. The heat is overwhelming and everyone is feeling it. Everywhere we go at present people say it is not usually so hot. And then it occurs to me that the daily temperatures printed in the English newspapers we buy are never as high as those on our new thermometer, despite our being in one of the actual cities quoted. I begin to wonder where these figures come from. I also realize that the electronic displays they have in the streets, whose LED screen tells the time and the temperature alternately, don't tell the temperature any more, as if they don't want anybody to know. And with your hair steaming in the heat you ask waspishly where the thermometer that produces the temperatures in the newspapers is actually kept—in the Minister of Tourism's basement?

37

Ibiza

With the acquisition of a new radio, the contents of our saloon washed and dried and our water tanks full—the last-mentioned being the only thing we actually came to Palma for—we set off for our original destination. Ibiza. It is a bouncy journey, against the wind with a fair chop to the sea, but once tucked into the island's small bays conditions are perfect for lazing and swimming. At one anchorage, though, the sound of dragging is so strong through the boat that David dives down to our anchor. It is well dug in but the sound persists. It is quite some time before we work out that a full starboard water tank, set in motion by a specific sea state, gives a very convincing impersonation of an anchor dragging.

We intend to journey on to Ibiza's capital but a strong south-westerly wind is forecast. It will make the anchorages there uncomfortable, and to stay where we are now is not a good idea either. So, as often happens when cruising, you find yourself going in the opposite direction to the one you intended simply in order to find somewhere sheltered and safe. We choose Cala Charraca and stay there two days, lazing and swimming while waiting for a strong south-westerly which never arrives. We also e-mail our newsletter to family and friends who have computers, and print out again the copies ruined by seawater for those who don't.

AFTER A COUPLE OF days we decide to resume our journey, only to find that in spite of a new and propitious forecast we are soon chopping into a strong head wind that is not supposed to be there. Nevertheless, we finally arrive at Ibiza Harbor. The Old Town looks lovely up on its hill. As for anchoring, however, the harbor reminds us of London's M25 motorway on a Friday evening but with a perpetual wash from ferries thrown in.

However, a narrow strip of land separates the harbor from a large shallow bay called Cala Talamanca. There are a few catamarans already anchored there and we join them. The water is aquamarine as I steer over patches of pale yellow sand and silvery-green weed until David finds a suitably large patch of sand to drop the anchor in.

We are getting low on fresh foodstuffs by now although we still have five lemons, six heads of garlic and quite a few leeks. We have no desire, on a hot afternoon, to dinghy ashore, walk two miles into town, spend an hour or so gathering supplies and then walk two miles back with them. We have wine and chocolate for lunch which is quite disgraceful but utter bliss. And we have dinner on the beach, with the water lapping two inches below the edge of the restaurant's wooden terrace.

For a Northerner there is something captivating about the Mediterranean's lack of tide; to be able to build your house or set out your tables so close to water with confidence. There are no guarantees against speed freaks of course and, when one does roar past, a surge of water breaches the terrace at one side and exits at the other. Its passage is diner-friendly, however, running as it does behind the rear tables and across the restaurant's doorway; requiring the waiters to step over it as they cross the threshold, but missing the diners altogether.

NEXT MORNING WE TAKE the dinghy ashore very early and walk the two miles into town. The city of Ibiza was founded by the Carthaginians who are also thought to have fortified the hill known as *D'Alt Vila*, The Old Town, and to have called both it and the island *Ibasim*. Ibiza then became a Roman city state and Hannibal is said to have been born on a small island off its west coast. When the Moors came they called it *Yebisah*. The Vikings and later Charlemagne looted and pillaged it. The walls enclosing the upper, or old town, were built in the 16th century under Emperor Charles V.

We climb the hill to The Old Town, wandering through the castle with its wonderful views over the town and bays, and visiting the cathedral with its massive 13th century belfry. The cathedral is wonderfully cool after the shimmering heat outside. There is an official sitting at a table against the west wall as you enter. Although perfectly upright he is fast asleep and all the people coming in and going out, as though with a shared thought, tiptoe past the table to avoid disturbing him.

We lunch on sangria and tapas in the shade of a huge, gnarled old olive tree. Then we shop and post our newly reprinted newsletter. The little yellow metal post box is inside a tobacconist's shop. Nobody we'd asked was sure where the actual post office is hidden, although somebody had said it was a day's hike out of town.

We return to a very hot dinghy with our shopping. The wind is rising and there is some cloud. The weed beneath us, once silvery green, is now dark grey and the sandy patches a lurid lime green. It is a little eerie, sometimes, the way the sea's colors change when the weather does.

38

Formentera

Our next destination, the little island of Formentera, is only eleven miles from Ibiza so it is not surprising that its history is similar. Its name derives from *Frumentaria*, a reference to the large amount of wheat it supplied to the Roman Empire. It was raided by all the usual suspects plus the Saracens and, ironically, Scandinavians on their way home from a crusade.

In its modern incarnation the island has a tiny town, a very loud disco and an enormously long, beautiful sandy beach. The latter contains a mud bath—not mentioned in the cruising guide—in which people immerse themselves totally in grey mud and then walk slowly along the beach until it dries, peels and drops off like rotting flesh. It is quite appalling, surrounded as you are by tanned healthy bodies, to be suddenly confronted by something out of *Return of the Zombies*. Given that the beach is popular for all-night revels, a glimpse of one of these mud bathers after dark would probably unhinge anyone of a nervous disposition.

THE ANCHORAGE IS GUNWALE-TO-GUNWALE with yachts. Late afternoon it seems to have achieved saturation point when seven middle-aged Germans on a charter Benetteau roar up, drop their anchor between two of us, ride over it at speed, turn on the radio full blast, take off all their clothes, throw themselves into the sea, talk at the tops of their voices, and have a lanyard clattering against their mast so loudly it would drive any normal person demented, but which they don't seem to notice.

Then a 50-foot motor yacht arrives with eight men on deck dancing in pairs, cheek-to-cheek, while their skipper races about desperately trying to anchor unassisted in a very confined space. This boat's dance music can not compete with the Benetteau's very loud radio, however, let alone the rave on the shore.

After the disco in the town finishes around dawn, dozens of people arrive on the beach and sing, for hours, and what really impresses us is that they know all the words of every song.

We have the little town largely to ourselves next morning since most people have only recently gone to bed. But when we return to collect our dinghy, the spot on the quay where we had tied it up is now taken by a dive boat. Our dinghy had been untied and left to float away. Fortunately, it has been rescued by a fellow-yachtsman.

Formentera is undoubtedly a very nice place when it is not so crowded. But this is high season and we are happy to leave.

Mainland Spain

39

Alicante

W e leave the Balearics for mainland Spain on Friday the Thirteenth, destination Alicante. We are up before dawn and set off at first light. It is a very beautiful morning. Layers of soft gray Ibizan mountains recede into a smoky distance, while above them light cloud reflects the red glow of a sun not quite risen. Four and a half hours later we can still look back and see Ibiza, but Formentera is such a low-lying island that it disappeared from sight long ago.

Around 6pm the wind disappears but we leave the genoa up as a sunshade for the cockpit. It gets dark around nine o'clock. We enter Alicante marina just before midnight and tie up to the fuel dock until the reception staff arrives for work next morning and allocates us a berth. It is a very warm night and we opt for separate bunks so that we can sprawl like beached starfish under an open hatch. David takes port, and I take starboard, beside the quay.

At 4.45am—and remembering to put on some clothing—I go up on deck, point to the alarm clock in my left hand and say, 'Look Guys,' to three youths and a girl singing and chatting two feet from my bed. They are doing it very amiably but, after an hour and a half, enough is enough. And why do four young people want to sit around diesel pumps when Alicante has a beautiful promenade? Security, probably, at this time of the morning, but it is none of my business now they have stopped singing next to my bed. And then I feel guilty. It is the difference between holiday-makers with a short time in which to enjoy themselves and people like us. They are young and, unlike us, have only a couple of weeks to enjoy warm nights full of stars. But I have just spent nineteen hours at sea and the Battle of the Lavandaria looms again tomorrow.

As SOON AS RECEPTION opens at 9am I buy four laundry tokens and rush off with a load, only to find both washing machines already in use. I place my bags on the table as next in line and return to the fuel dock to help David berth Voyager in the finger pontoon he has been allocated. I don't know which is worse, a lazy line or finger pontoons with their little pointy ends always sneaking between your fenders and gouging their way into your topsides.

By the time I get back to the launderette, one of the machines has almost completed its cycle and a newly-arrived Italian woman is plainly expecting to put her washing in next. I, however, was trained here, by Annie from Humberside, and begin to explain the concept of standing in line to her. Given last year's experience I am going to spend the whole of today in this launderette, but unless I stand my ground I am likely to spend much of tomorrow here as well.

She protests but I am bigger than she is and finally I spell it out to her in terms she cannot fail to understand. 'Me *primo*,' I say, jabbing my right thumb at my collarbone. 'You *secondus*.' I've just got her pacified when the Scotsman whose machine is rightfully mine presses the green button for *start* instead of the yellow button to open the door. Its lock slams into place and the machine starts a full wash cycle going again for another hour. In the meantime a Portuguese couple arrives with a huge holdall, the male half of the pair exhibiting every indication that he expects to use the next machine that falls vacant.

So I decide to soften him up by telling him about my laundry experience with the Portuguese Navy last year when we got chased by a frigate for having my nightie hanging over the side. I'm hooting away but it's going down like a lead balloon. On reflection there is a bit of the naval look about him and I remember that Portuguese men from some areas have this macho thing about women and not much of a sense of humor anyway and it is all becoming a bit fraught. An international incident even, with Little England ranged against the combined EU forces of Italy and Portugal. With the prospect of a second day tied to this hot, airless room, however, Little England holds her ground, parlies, outlines the concept of standing in line, negotiates an ethical washing machine policy, entente cordiale is maintained and the man goes away.

Freed from his brooding presence, it turns out that the Italian woman comes from a little town on the coast near Rome and her son works for British Telecom. The Portuguese woman teaches literature and the time passes pleasurably as she talks about her favorite authors.

After they have gone I go and buy a small beer from the restaurant next door and sit in the sunshine. It is at times like this that you miss cigarettes. You can't leave your laundry and go and do something useful because when you return you will be fifth in line, so you just sit and wait and as one load finishes you throw in the next.

Meanwhile, David heroically sets off to shop, promising me faithfully he will come back by taxi since El Corte Inglés is quite a long way up into the town and I know he will return with as much as it is possible to carry. He is dressed in old tracksuit bottoms with a broken pocket zip and an elderly T-shirt; the only clean clothes left in his locker as everything else is in bags in the launderette with me. He leaves El Corte Inglés's air-conditioning with regret, a very large rucksack full to bursting and numerous carrier bags.

Despite his attire David has received nothing but courtesy from the store's staff but fails to impress the taxi driver. David indicates the marina on the map to the man, who looks puzzled and mutters in Spanish. David keeps repeating 'Marina, marina,' and pointing to its location on the map, and they set off.

At the waterfront the driver tries to take David past the marina to holiday apartments and David insists he turn into the service road to the marina instead—which he does, at top speed through two busy lanes of traffic. But he then tries to deliver him to the Algerian ferry whose terminal shares the service road with the marina and which is boarding at that moment with lots of people dressed like David and carrying polybags and cardboard boxes.

David clearly does not fit the driver's stereotype of a yacht-owner. He makes him stop the taxi before he enters the terminal, pays and gets out. Then, overloaded with shopping he has to trudge round a huge complex of buildings to get back into the marina.

Four loads of washing finally get finished at 3pm and fill the boat's rails twice over. I can't be bothered waiting for the dryer.

WE GET UP AT first light Sunday morning, wash Voyager down with soapy water and hose her off. Then we do her bright work with that cream cleaner most people have under their kitchen sink. The stuff you buy in a chandlery to polish a boat's chrome and stainless steel costs fifteen times as much as a bottle of sink scrub which is just as good. Then there is the ironing and letters to write.

We go to the post office and the market next morning. As the fresh fish stalls are closed on Mondays we had planned to buy chicken upstairs, but while buying fruit, vegetables and bread on the ground floor we notice a stall selling sardines in bulk. The stall holder is a charming man and gives us a third of a kilo (sixteen sardines and enough for a good plateful each tonight) in exchange for a 100 peseta coin or 40pence.

Back at the marina we top up our water tanks, return our shower block key and water connecter to reception and despite a brisk wind make a rather stylish exit, only there is no-one about. There never is when you do anything well, only when you mess it up horribly. It is sunny but cool on the move and the wind quickly shifts round to the nose.

40

Tabarca

A fter Alicante, our intended destination is Torreviejo but we have traveled only eight miles when the sea becomes so bumpy and uncomfortable that we decide to anchor in the shelter of a tiny fortified island,
the Isle de Tabarca, and see if it settles overnight. This is the island we had
passed one Saturday afternoon last year on our way east. At that time it
had been bristling with visiting fishermen, hemmed in by rows of pleasure
boats and swarming with visitors constantly arriving by ferry. None of
them is here now so, early next morning, we go ashore.

Several centuries ago this island was a base for pirates. After they were
finally driven out, a small fortified village was built and garrisoned to
prevent further occupation. Its defensive walls, small fort and surprisingly
large church dedicated to St Peter, are crumbling now, but made picturesque by palm and pine trees and red bougainvillea. The villagers live fru-
gally from fishing, as they have always done, and quite isolated from the
material abundance of mainland Spain just three short miles away.

Touchingly, as you pass through the gateway in the great stone defensive wall there is a rough street plan to guide you, although there are
only a handful of tiny streets. They are unsealed, but there are no vehicles
anyway. The village square is only differentiated from the roads around it
by a neat line of carefully-laid stones and terracotta pots with little palms
in them.

The terraced houses are small and neat with lace curtains at the windows and, despite the earliness of the hour, the women are already out
sweeping the tiled sidewalks in front of their homes and the dirt roads
beyond them. Heaven knows what it must be like for dust here when

the wind really blows, but it is noticeable at the tiny café where we have our breakfast that the cash register is wrapped in cling film. Flags are out in the streets and a bier, the sort on which four men carry a saint's statue through the streets, lies on the ground outside the church as if a festival has recently taken place.

The people that you pass meet your eyes, consider you briefly and then greet you courteously; impressive in a place that spends much of its time deluged in gawping visitors. The cats are wary, but the dogs have no interest in strangers at all and hurry about their business. They all resemble each other, with curly fur and amiable faces, as if long ago an Airedale had fraternized with something smaller and more cheerful. Below the walls the fishermen who have spent the night out on the rocks are wading back to the village with their bedrolls balanced on their heads. We leave the island and return to the boat with a sense of having stepped back in time.

41

The Costas

The sea is calm now after yesterday's agitation so we resume our journey to Torreviejo, which will be our last harbor until we reach Gibraltar. After Torreviejo we simply drop anchor each evening in a deserted bay, for although it is mid-August there is hardly anybody about. This is because the Costas are not cruising grounds, there being few sheltered anchorages. We are simply lucky that the weather is being kind to us.

As the bays are deserted at night, so is the shoreline by day. This absence of Homo sapiens heightens the sense of the primeval, for we are sailing down the edge of a land that once erupted as molten rock. In so doing, it created a coastline of extraordinary colors and textures. There is white rock like whipped cream adjacent to mocha coffee; pale greens and soft browns dotted with bleached scrub that looks from a distance like cotton wool balls; lumpy black is fused with smooth grey; yellow that looks as if it rose from the sea the texture of butter on a warm day, arced and set; and grim volcanic grey, harsh as pumice, nudges soft eroding cream that seems illuminated from within, as if sunlight has been trapped inside it.

In one place caves make huge gashes in the cliffs at sea level. In another, the upper cliff face is pocked by what look from out at sea like niches in a church wall. A handful of fishermen have scrambled down from the cliff top to stand in them, like plaster saints, protecting themselves from the furnace-blast of the mid-day August sun with large striped umbrellas.

In a deserted bay, 19th century industrial architecture crumbles. Apart from a wondrous circular building, only facades remain standing, stately and classical, among the spoil of opencast mining.

These deserted stretches of coastline are the more surprising because

159

they are part of the Costa Blanca and the Costa del Sol, two of Europe's major holiday destinations. Yet, from the sea, the resorts which make them famous are negligible. They are simply part of a larger landscape, their teeming beaches bordered by others which are empty, or by deserted coves and spectacular cliffs and, all the while, behind them, are the towering peaks of the sierras.

Ahead of us, in the distance, dark, languid shapes appear in the water, followed by the sound of rushing air. Whales break the surface, sending great plumes of water rushing out of the blowholes on the top of their heads. They sink slowly back into the water again as we get close to them only to re-appear in our wake. After a few times you realize their appearance ahead of you is not a co-incidence. They wait there for you to arrive and then sink so that you pass over them. Perhaps the churning water from a boat's propellers is pleasurable. Or maybe they are simply curious.

And it is along this coast that we first become aware of another activity in the water, one that is inexplicable. A fin first, then a glimpse of a round silvery underside. The fin appears to be waving.

42

Tranquil Anchorages

Cala Bardina, our first anchorage on this enchanting coast, is not even named on our chart. David will find its name in a library atlas long afterwards. We arrive early evening, have dinner in the cockpit and look out on a very beautiful bay. There is a stunning building of which Bavaria's castle-mad King Ludwig might have approved, all ups and downs and terracotta roofs. Its glistening whiteness is set off by dark green palm trees and its golden lights shine out against the darkness of the hills behind it.

Our second night's anchorage is called Puerto de Genovés although it is not a port at all, just a sheltered beach with the odd villa. Nearby San José, however—while not suitable as an anchorage that night—has a village, so next morning we stop off there in search of fresh food.

We drop anchor and David rows us ashore. A sea swell, combined with a shoaling beach, is producing surf and we approach the sand in a flurry of white water. Surf is no problem so long as David balances the dinghy with the oars, and I leap out fast and drag it onto firm sand before the receding surf can drag it backwards, turn it sideways and tip it over.

The village, just above the beach, has a supermarket whose current refurbishment has turned it temporarily into an object lesson in collision chaos and customer stress. People entering are immediately confronted by customers with shopping carts waiting to go through the checkout, and have to struggle through them to get inside. As you move through the supermarket you irrevocably arrive at its centre, which is a narrow passage containing a long counter at which you join one of three separate lines depending on whether you want fresh meat, cooked meats or cheese. The service here is slow, given all the traditional parcel wrapping, and lines of shoppers fill the passage. Unfortunately the congestion is exacerbated by the fact that at present this is also the only route to the checkout, where you again become part of the scrum between shoppers waiting to pay and newcomers trying to get in through the door.

Before we began cruising, and with both of us working full time, David did our weekly shop-up for years. I worked miles from a decent supermarket while there was a splendid one around the corner from David's office. He was, he said, also better equipped in the spinal department to stand in checkout lines and load and unload heavy bags, and I never argued. Like most men who shop, however, he liked to do it fast. Familiarity with the store's layout meant he could shop, with an eye to freshness and economy, for the whole week in 30 minutes from entering the doors to unloading his cart at the checkout. He had no interest in browsing and on the few occasions I accompanied him would become quite impatient if I paused to look at anything not on the shopping list and begin herding me ahead of him with his cart.

The lines at the meat and cheese counters now prove too much for him. 'We're only shopping for *one day*,' he says, edging carefully around tiny ladies dressed in black as he navigates his way to the seething checkout. 'The day after tomorrow we'll be at a place with a big supermarket.'

David has always been an optimist. I tend to err on the side of caution and like to have plenty put by for emergencies. It is not unknown for us to head for somewhere the cruising guide recommends as 'ideal for re-provisioning' only to find that either we cannot anchor there for some reason, or the weather makes it impossible to go ashore. Then we are off again at dawn the next day, as like as not to a deserted bay. I squeeze between the grid-locked shopping carts and follow him.

Stumbling from the checkout onto the street we discover a pastry shop by following its heavenly smell. Crossing its threshold, however, is like walking into an oven, yet unbelievably it is also a café. Several people are sitting at tables but seem torpid in the heat. Drenched in perspiration and our lungs hot, we stagger back outside into a comparatively tepid 90°F clutching a meat pie, a cheese and ham lattice and fruit slices.

We load the dinghy for the trip back to Voyager, our fragrant cargo balanced amidships. David gets in and splays the oars while I push us out from the beach. It doesn't take any strength on my part. I just need to time it so that the dinghy clears the surf created by the shoaling beach, David gets a good pull on the oars into clear water, I jump in and we're on our way.

Today, however, instead of springing lightly in over the stern I misjudge the exact place where the sand shoals. My right foot fails to connect with solid ground and falling sideways I end up scrambling into the dinghy the best way I can. I lie face down, half in and half out, surprised that even half of me has made it. The dinghy, made unstable by my lower half hanging over its port quarter, bucks like a bronco in the surf and tries to turn sideways. David meanwhile is looking anxiously behind him, to ensure that he is keeping the dinghy at right angles to the breaking waves that will otherwise capsize us.

'At least get in the middle!' he snaps with uncharacteristic irritation, unaware that my inert body is about to disappear overboard. At that moment, however, a large breaker hits us, the stern jolts upwards, and I slide into the bottom of the dinghy like a landed fish. Happily I miss the meat pie, which we have for lunch, still warm, with salad, crusty bread and a rough red wine.

43

Sea Mist

....

Our anchorage tonight is Punta de los Baños, a shallow bay on the end of a point, or *punta* of land with an old castle to our left and a small lighthouse to our right. We arrive early evening. On the beach a young man with deadly earnest slaps, snaps, stretches, kneads, pulls and pummels a perspiring friend into a wetsuit too small for him. Only when the friend is hauled onto his feet, limbs stuck out sideways like a dried starfish and his face the color of a ripe tomato, does the young man accept defeat and set about stripping him again.

There is a large red sunset behind a large brown hill. At dusk the rock fishermen drift silently down the beach and settle themselves for the night. A light below its walls makes the old castle hauntingly beautiful against the darkness. The small lighthouse seems to be lit with a 30-watt bulb. It is a clear, windless night. The sea laps against the rocks below the fishermen's feet, and over our stern steps as we rock gently in a slight sea swell.

There is heavy dew overnight and next morning it covers our decks and forms large glistening dewdrops in long even lines under every horizontal surface. As we move about the cockpit, preparing to leave, they drip from the boom and the edges of the wheel house roof onto our heads and down the back of our necks. The whole boat glitters like a jeweled thing in the morning light. Tiny droplets of moisture illuminate the webs of the modest little spiders who weave their normally-invisible little larders underneath our rails, girding Voyager's sides in the finest gossamer. The davits, dinghy and back stays, colonized by larger species, are strung with diamond necklaces.

We raise the anchor and set off in a great red sunrise. The sea is glossy and sinuous in the early morning mist. There is no horizon and in the distance tiny fishing boats hang suspended in the shining blueness. As we move offshore the mist distorts even David's spatial awareness and neither of us has the remotest idea of just how much visibility we have. We turn on the radar and find that the shore we have recently left, and which we can still just see, is actually over a mile away which is further than either of us had thought.

Small day boats rarely show up on radar, and fishing buoys never do, so I keep watch on the foredeck through mile after mile of blue-gray sea and the strange silvery light that the sun becomes when filtered through mist. Fish leap en masse and mid-morning dolphins arrive. There are seven of them. They slide back and forth under our hulls and swim between our bows, diving under and over each other. You never become blasé about them and always feel sorry when they leave.

After watching for such a long time in this unrelenting brightness, tiny silver lights begin pinging behind my eyes. When, some time later, these are joined by irregular grey patches, I think it is probably time to go and have a lie down. Even as the thought is forming, however, I find myself yelling, 'Whales! Slow down! We'll hit them!'

We have no idea what most of them are and never encounter such a mixed bunch so close to us again. It is likely that the reason we have done so this morning is that they are resting after feeding and in the heavy mist have been caught unawares.

By the time Voyager comes to a halt we are among them and a mass of large startled bodies scatter in all directions. Long grey whales arc slowly away blowing great plumes of water through their blow holes as they go. Something 20 feet long, pale and flat with a mottled back and frilly edges, slides away beneath us. Some I recognize as bottlenose dolphins, only bigger than we have ever encountered before. Less cautious than the whales, instead of bolting they hover a short way off and once we increase our speed again come rushing back to swim between our hulls, turning their heads on one side to observe us leaning over the rails. Dolphins never miss an opportunity and, after the serious business of digestion, it's *playtime*.

EVERY ONCE IN A while the sun burns through the mist and wispy clouds are reflected in the flat water. Sometimes the mist is so dense there is no sun at all and visibility is reduced to only a few yards beyond the boat. I finally get to shout 'Land ho!', however, as the brown peaks of the Sierra Nevada become visible and we change course for our destination.

Gradually the mist lifts from the sea. It is littered with small fishing boats, the first vessels we have seen in five hours. The mist also lifts from the land, except for a deep blue band obscuring the waterfront altogether so that we look out upon four distinct stripes: bright shiny sea, deep blue mist, brown mountains, blue hazy sky.

44

A Secluded Bay

....

Nerja, the anchorage we have earmarked for tonight's stop, and where the cruising guide says that supplies are available, turns out to be a teeming beach and holiday complex. With all the jet skis, pedalos, sailing dinghies and roaring little motor boats we decide to give it a miss and a mile further along the coast find a small bay. It has only a couple of day boats in it, and an open wooden boat with a large canvas parasol in the middle and a man with a fishing rod at either end. We drop our anchor.

It could not be more different from the bay we have just left. Rising vertically from the small beach is a cliff, with a terraced hillside on top. There is an ancient, single-storey house among the terraces with a vine above its door and windows. A narrow path passes the house from the beach below to an unseen road at the top of the cliff.

The beach itself, with rocks at either end and little depth, is more like a marine garden than a beach. There is lots of greenery and large cacti cascading down the cliff face and in one corner a family has created a multi-colored summer house from beach towels, sarongs and beach mats. It has chairs and a makeshift table and all the accoutrements of eating out of doors. At the other end of the beach a couple in blue swim-wear lie supine under blue umbrellas beside a small blue and white circular tent. Few have come unencumbered and no-one moves much all afternoon. It is Saturday and the locals are at their leisure, inclined to rest rather than frolic.

It is equally relaxed and pleasant where we are, among the other anchored boats. A couple of children swim lazily, a couple of adolescents flirt in a desultory sort of way, but mostly people laze in the sun, until around 6pm when the jet skis arrive and roar round and round in relatively small circles. The water is quickly churned into a frenzy, the air filled with the stench of exhaust fumes, and the peace shattered by the whine of their engines and the roll from their wash. And you think about the generations who have worked the terraced hillside above and raised families in the old house and lived quiet lives above a quiet bay until the late 20th century invented purposeless noise and motion.

By seven the jet skis have gone and peace resumes. When the sun sinks below the cliff-top the people on the beach begin to carry vast loads of chairs, drinks coolers, water carriers, bedrolls, beach mats and tents up the steep path past the old single-storey house. With the cliff now in shade, someone leaves the house and goes up onto the terraces to weed and water the neat rows of plants. We are still in sunshine; just us and some fruit flies, for the other boats have also left, including the wooden fishing boat with the big canvas umbrella. We have dinner, swat fruit flies and contemplate our GPS.

All current GPS units have been working to a calendar for a set number of years, with an expiry date this year on August 22—tomorrow—after which the newer models will automatically re-set themselves. No GPS manufacturer mentioned an expiry date until a year or so ago and if your unit cost several thousand pounds, as ours did, the news came as an unpleasant shock.

Our GPS is five years old and, unsure if it is a newer or an older generation model, and not wanting to be caught without it, David contacted the manufacturer a year ago to find out. They assured him that it would re-set itself. There were, however, so many stories in the yachting magazines—including fears that even some very recent models would not re-set themselves automatically—that he had checked with the manufacturer again a few months later, in case anything had changed. He was again reassured that ours would re-set itself.

Throughout the day something has waved a fin above the water. It has shone and glittered and seagulls have sat around and watched it. Now it disappears. Will our GPS do likewise, we wonder, on the morrow?

The answer is: Yes. The manufacturer's assertion that our GPS would survive the roll-over date is contradicted by its own equipment. This morning it is as dead as a dodo. As a precaution we have already dug out a hand-held Magellan GPS which David bought last year as a backup.

However, for simplicity we just turn Voyager's stern to the beach and head out to sea in a straight line using the compass.

We leave just before nine in heavy mist and everywhere is absolutely dripping. I watch from the foredeck for a while as a precaution. Visibility is so poor and confusing that at one stage we prepare to change course for what turns out to be a jumbo-size bleach bottle floating on the surface.

Then a large family of common dolphins stops by. They are exuberant and quite competitive, with the occasional synchronized leap but mostly freestyle. Common dolphins are smaller than the more-familiar bottlenose, have a less-pronounced beak, but are a real joy. They are beautifully marked, with a figure-8 pattern on their flanks, fast and athletic. They are also very responsive to human presence and go out of their way to attract your attention.

Sometime later David eyes the galley and asks suspiciously, 'What's for lunch? This is the man who chivvied me out of a supermarket the day before yesterday saying, 'We're only shopping for *one day!*' These are the times you get out the cans and bottles. We have tuna in tartare sauce with capers and olives, plus the last of the cheese, lettuce, tomato and four pieces of surprisingly fresh brown bread.

There is an African Kikuyu proverb: *Never throw anything away until you have something of value to replace it.* These days I never feed the birds with the end of a loaf until I have my hands on a fresh one. However, when this has gone … I ruminate on coming days. We still have four lemons left from El Corte Inglés and quite a bit of garlic. Not appetizing on their own perhaps but, famed as lemon and garlic are for their antiseptic qualities, at least our intestinal flora will be thoroughly disinfected.

The sun finally makes its way through the mist after lunch and finishes drying what the wind has not yet got around to. It also brings out other vessels and it is like driving a car on a country road: nothing for miles and then suddenly, all together, there's a parked van, a cyclist, and somebody walking a dog on your side of the road and just as you pull out to overtake them a semi-trailer comes round the bend in front of you. At the moment it is several fishing dinghies drifting aimlessly, plus two power boats, and another yacht heading directly at us. There is also a raft of sewage and assorted garbage that we really do not want to sail through. When the sea is flat like this you can see just how much rubbish lies about.

Unfortunately, the world treats the sea as a giant trash can and expects whatever is thrown into it to disappear. It doesn't. It just goes somewhere else. Traditionally coastal towns and cities have routinely dumped their garbage into the sea. Some still do. So have cruise ships.

The worst offenders are plastic and nylon. Even a plastic composite milk carton takes an estimated five years to break down. A supermarket polybag between 10 and 20 years. Six-pack holder rings 450 years. Diapers 500 to 800 years. But plastic bottles, styrofoam cups and discarded fishing net last for ever.

It is difficult to know whether plastic thrown into the sea is less dangerous when it does finally degrade or when it does not. When it breaks down, it still doesn't go away. It becomes chemical molecules that poison the marine environment.

Intact, it is a constant threat to wildlife. For instance, it is surprising how often you see those shiny, purple, heart-shaped party balloons bobbing about on the open sea with most of their helium gone. And a regular feature is supermarket polybags, pulsating just below the surface as they are pushed along by the tide. Unfortunately, both are ingested by unwary sea turtles who mistake them for a staple part of their diet—jellyfish. Sadly, the plastic blocks their digestive tract and they die.

And those plastic rings which hold six-packs of canned drinks together are just the right size to slide over an inquisitive dolphin's beak. Once there it holds the mouth closed and the dolphin starves to death. An estimated one million seabirds a year choke, drown or starve because of discarded nets and other debris, along with hundreds of thousands of seals, sea lions, whales, dolphins, sharks and sea turtles.

There is quite a bit of pollution above us, too, of the noise and aviation fuel variety, for we are now under the flight path for Malaga airport. Our serene voyage along this stunning coastline is at an end, although there is still fin-waving everywhere.

45

Marbella

Early evening we try to get into Marbella marina.
'Completo,' shouts an attendant from an over-crowded pontoon and cheerfully waves us away.

We anchor off the beach. It is a most attractive waterfront of large villas with the most beautiful gardens of sub-tropical trees and evergreens. All around us it is bedlam. The half dozen super yachts, anchored out in deeper water, have dispatched their fleets of jet skis and riders and they are roaring round and round inshore. The cruiser's natural enemies are fishermen and rich people.

The noise is horrendous; the smell worse. Petrol fumes lie over the water in a gray haze, like a motorway on a humid day. The stench in the nostrils is so acrid that we go below and close our doors and hatches, but too late to prevent David sneezing. Battening down proves to be a good move for another reason, as jets of seawater from their exhausts fly over our boat. I have no desire to lose any more belongings or spend any more time washing seawater from carpets and upholstery.

I should also be most unhappy, I reflected, had I bought an idyllic waterfront villa here only to languish indoors behind double glazing and air-conditioning because of other people's noise and fumes.

Meanwhile, in the greenhouse conditions inside an airless Voyager, the fruit flies multiply. Their continued presence is a mystery. I keep spraying, yet there is never any reduction in their numbers. There is no fruit on board, apart from lemons and they are sitting in style in an almost empty fridge. Nor is there anything else lying about for them to live on. Except … The thought occurs to both of us at the same time.

Throughout our odyssey along a largely deserted coast there has been nowhere suitable to dispose of our refuse so our dinghy has been doing service as a dumpster. As soon as the jet skis return to the super yachts we go outside and contemplate the collection of gash bags lying in our dinghy. The bags hum, in both senses of the word. David carries them to the forward locker and shuts them up in there.

By 8.30 almost everybody has gone but us, the air is fresh again and it is bliss. We have just dined on pasta. The coffee pot is in the cockpit. The sun is setting behind the lovely trees sheltering the expensive villas and all the chairs on the beach are empty now—just a woman and a small child at the water's edge, reluctant to leave.

Everywhere is perfectly still. There is a three-quarter moon and a distant, solitary fishing boat floats in space because the sea and the sky are the same color and the eye cannot find a horizon against which to place it.

SOME TIME LATER I detect a faint rubbery smell when I go into the starboard cabin. David goes in, sniffs and says, 'Hmm'. He is always dismissive about my sense of smell because he has very little himself, whereas I wonder sometimes if I might have been a bloodhound in a former life.

We are uneasy in the night and get up around 2am to check our location, but Voyager is lying exactly where we left her, parallel to the beach and facing west. There is no wind despite a forecast for gentle to moderate breezes from the east. Visibility is clear. The yellow lamps along the waterfront shine brightly, illuminating the lovely trees in the gardens of the villas above the beach in a way that is quite magical.

A few minutes later we cannot see the beach at all and even the yellow lamps are barely visible. It is so sudden and creepy it reminds me of the arrival of the leper ship in *The Fog*. The film is set in a small town on the US coast of Maine whose current prosperity stems from the gold the town's founders accepted from a group of lepers in exchange for refuge for their ship. The townspeople, however, had betrayed the lepers and as the film opens the rotting hulk of their ghost ship drifts silently in with a sea fog and its ghostly crew is about to unleash a horrifying revenge upon the founders' descendents.

Of more immediate concern, however, is being hit by a fishing trawler. My worry is that we are not in a bay but on a long coastline with small outcrops. However, as David points out, the fish dock is well away from us and any boats leaving or entering it are unlikely to come this close to shore. It is that old intuition thing again. I know we have a problem waiting to happen, but I don't know what it is. Nevertheless we return to bed and go back to sleep.

At daybreak, when we start the engines ready for another foggy departure, the starboard engine's alternator warning light comes on. David suspects a broken fan belt but when he lifts the lid he finds the engine bay half-full of sea water. The water inlet hose has broken away from its retaining strap and the fan belt wheel has rubbed through it: that faint rubbery smell I detected yesterday. The result is that seawater is flowing in through the ruptured hose and the fan belt is spraying it all over the engine and electrics. David turns off the engine, closes the stopcock to prevent us sinking and we begin baling out.

46

Marbella to Gibraltar

We set off through the fog on one engine. David had set a compass bearing the previous night and we have the radar on. Originally we had never thought about having radar. Until we bought Voyager we had never even been on a yacht that had it. It just happened to be on the boat when we bought her. Now we wouldn't be without it.

Steering 175°, almost due south, by the manual compass we follow a straight line until we are about a mile from shore and clear of all obstructions. It is then safe to turn west and resume our journey to Gibraltar. I take what has become my usual morning place at the bow rail. The air is so moisture-laden that it drips like rain. I have to wipe a handkerchief across the lenses of my sunglasses every thirty seconds or so to see through them. Take them off and the fog mists your eyes, droplets gather on your lashes and the glare is unbearable. My hair is dripping and my feet are soggy.

When we are well out to sea David sets the autopilot but finds that its compass read-out is different from the manual one. After comparing the Magellan hand-held GPS against both of them he finds that it corresponds to the manual compass, so the fault must lie with the autopilot. David hates mysteries, especially of the technological kind, and there is a great deal of thought and fiddling going on at the helm. Out on the foredeck I suspect I might have the beginnings of trench foot.

Unfortunately, David's contemplation of the autopilot detracts from his contemplation of the radar. I have just wiped a soggy handkerchief across my lenses for the thousandth time when the leper ship looms at me through the fog. I turn to David, but he is not looking. I begin jumping up and down and waving; shouting at him to look up, see the boat and

174

alter course. The young fisherman on our port side had clearly been paying attention to his own radar, knew we would pass safely, and mistaking my hysteria for a greeting waves back. He glides past, only yards from us, and disappears immediately back into the fog.

The mystery of the autopilot compass reading is finally solved. Our portable radio had been left on the floor of the saloon beside the sofa. The sofa has a locker underneath it, in the corner of which—only inches from where the radio lies—is the fluxgate gyro compass which provides the autopilot's compass read-out at the helm. The magnet in the radio's speaker has affected the autopilot's compass by around 20%.

The autopilot is not the only thing on board to suffer from the effects of outside interference. The fog has deprived me of all sense of distance and relative size. A seagull dozing on the water, white-bodied with grey wings, becomes a distant boat with white topsides and grey superstructure. A small orange oceanographic survey buoy appears 15 feet tall.

When the fog thins temporarily, the sea takes on a soup bowl effect as if we are in a hollow and distant boats are on a rim, higher than we are. It is utterly disorientating to see a boat apparently sailing above the horizon. Once, turning back to face the bow again after a 360° check, I become convinced that we have made a sharp turn to port although David insists we have not wavered a degree in hours. A melancholy fog horn has been sounding for over an hour: two 10-second bursts followed by a minute and a half's silence. I can easily understand how lone sailors occasionally go mad. We have been staring into this shifting grayness since 7.30am and it is now noon.

Gradually the fog begins to lift. We get two separate visits from dolphins, first a group of common dolphins and then a family of bottlenose. I think that of all the pleasures of the sea the most captivating is dolphins. It is easy to understand their success in therapies for brain-damaged children for they transcend the mind and appeal to the spirit and the emotions. To be close to them is to experience pure joy. Today's prize for sheer panache, however, goes to the twenty-strong group of whatever it is that is doing the synchronized fin-waving within sight of a fishing trawler.

As we approach Gibraltar, half of the LCD display of our automatic steering disappears. We had spent hundreds of pounds having this repaired by the manufacturer before we returned to the Mediterranean in May. Now it would have to go back to England again, and we wonder how much of a delay this is going to cause. We do not want to set off on an Atlantic crossing without automatic steering. After leaving the Canaries we could be at sea for up to three weeks. With only two of us on board, it would be very tiring to have one or other of us constantly at the wheel. Hand-steering is particularly wearying at night, as your eyes constantly have to adjust between a lighted compass and the darkness around you.

As we limp towards Gib on one engine and minus our autopilot and our main GPS we ponder whether we should really be contemplating an Atlantic crossing at all, considering this level of equipment failure.

At least Navtex is working, although the level of warnings is so intimidating it is tempting to turn round and leave again. There are damaged navigational buoys and an oceanographic survey to worry about and the Army is hyperactive, with parachute jumping over here and gunnery practice over there. So if they don't survey you, jump on you or shoot you, you collide with a loose buoy without its top markings and, just to keep you on your toes, they've altered the markers inside one of the harbors. All this and only one engine.

It is flat calm to Europa Point, then windy once around it. As we pass the Governor's mansion, a number of fins are waving at us. The difference this time is that they are very close and we can see them clearly. Their fin-waving raises their flat round bodies out of the water a little and now we can see their pale undersides clearly for the first time. It is actually their face. It is a round, rather comical face and their vigorous waving seems to give it an animated expression as they gaze up at you.

We have only ever seen an artist's impression of them, on the faded marine-life posters you occasionally get in Iberia's coastal resorts, but finally we realize what they are—sun fish. Whatever purpose the fin waving serves for them, its effect on the viewer is rather like that of a welcoming committee, a marine equivalent of meeters and greeters.

Those other meeters and greeters—otherwise known as Immigration, Harbor Master and Customs—have had a change of staff since we called in here on our way into the Med, and are far more civil. Unlike last time though, when the wind was driving us remorselessly *off* the pontoon, it is now driving us *onto* it instead. So getting alongside, even with one engine out of action, is not a problem at all. Getting away again is.

Our catamaran has a propeller in each hull which means they are wide apart. This makes maneuvering in tight areas very easy. If, on the other hand, we are traveling in a relatively straight line it is also easy, not to say economical, to run with just one engine. However, if we need to maneuver, as now, with only one propeller and that propeller happens to be on the *inside* radius of the turn, the boat shows a marked reluctance to respond. And with an onshore wind and the starboard engine out of action, once we have completed the necessary paperwork David has no way of getting us off the customs dock except by me pushing with all my strength until the port propeller manages to persuade Voyager into a turn.

As she begins to leave the dock I jump aboard but unfortunately the wind proves too much and sends her back onto it. So I jump off and push again, but have barely had time to jump back on before the wind drives us dockside again. And so I keep leaping on and off and pushing until we finally manage to lurch away. Immigration and Harbor Master, meanwhile, both big men, come out and lean amiably on their doorway, with their muscular arms folded, to watch.

Gibraltar

47

Sheppards Boatyard

Since we are going to need a mechanic for the starboard engine, instead of the marina where we stayed last year we head for Sheppards Boatyard. A man with multiple tattoos, a wide smile and a Zapata moustache hauls us onto a pontoon despite the strong wind trying to blow us off it. This turns out to be Gaz, from England's south coast and unfailingly helpful. Because we don't know how long we might be held up getting repairs and replacements, Gaz finds us a slip at the cheaper end of the yard.

It is cheap because it is awaiting repair. Part of the concrete quay to which our wooden pontoon should be attached has begun to collapse and getting ashore requires a hop, skip and jump via a wobbly raft chained between the pontoon and a stable bit of concrete quay, followed by a scramble up a steel ladder. The electricity supply is eccentric, too, arriving via household 3-pin plugs stuck into a cable drum attached to a mains cable. We are simply grateful for the economy. Our in-boat equipment failure is going to be expensive.

Sheppard's Boatyard is a yachting institution; part of yachting history. It is also a friendly yard and consequently one of those places where people arrive for a brief stay and do not always leave again.

'Came for a holiday in '72,' says Jeff the mechanic, a cheerful Liverpudlian.

A desire to linger afflicts some of the berth holders too, like the catamaran opposite which sports Austrian blinds at its windows and fitted shag pile carpet on its cockpit sole.

Our first priority is the starboard engine. Happily Jeff announces that there is no damage from the sea water and while he sorts it out and then

181

services both engines ready for our voyage, David disconnects the relevant bit of the autopilot and sends it off to England by courier. Then he telephones England about our non-functioning GPS.

'Sorry,' says the manufacturer. 'We made a mistake. Your GPS won't re-start itself without a new program after all, but it's not economically viable for us to write new software to solve the problem. You'll have to buy a new one.'

David says it's not economically viable for us to buy another one of theirs and embarks on a search of marine catalogues and magazines for another brand. It arrives by post ten days later, at a fraction of the price of our original one, and with a computer screen containing a map which will show our position in relation to any coastline anywhere in the world. All we are waiting for now is the repair and return of our autopilot.

In the meantime we become acquainted with our neighbors. They include eight dogs, three cats, a wookie, a cockroach and possibly a vampire. Anywhere you find northern European women who have spent any time in Spain you will find rescue dogs. Five of these dogs and the three cats belong to a young Englishwoman called Jill on a black-hulled sloop at the end of our pontoon. She stops to introduce them one morning on their way out for exercise. As I extend a hand towards the nearest one she says, 'Mostly they're former hunting dogs. When the hunters have finished with them they dump them to starve.' Anticipating inbred savagery I withdraw my hand but caution proves unnecessary.

Four of them are short-haired, light brown hounds; three of which are lean and sleek, the fourth plump. Jill looks at the latter and sighs. 'After their hysterectomies she was the only one who put on weight.' The matronly one lowers her head and looks down at the pontoon apologetically. All four have that quietness noticeable in people and animals who have suffered deprivation and are grateful to have found a safe haven.

The fifth dog is Lucy, a fraction of their size, delicately boned, dark gray and furry. She has long legs supple as a spider's on which she dances rather than walks and she carries with her an aura of happiness. Looking at her it is impossible to guess what Lucy's parentage might have been. 'I found her in a bird cage on a market stall in Tenerife,' says Jill, 'when she was a few weeks old.'

Polite and patient they stand around us while we talk and when Jill walks away they troop after her single-file along the pontoon. They will pass thrice daily on their way to and from exercise and the rest of the time we neither see nor hear them. And they are so fastidious in their habits that they leave no trace of their passing on pontoon or dock. Lucy always brings up the rear during their outings and will not pass without offering her own personal greeting. Her small face lights up with pleasure at seeing you, while her body twists and turns and her nimble legs dance on the spot. Courtesies complete, she rushes off to catch up with her pack.

THE BOAT OPPOSITE US contains an older Englishwoman called Margaret. She has three dogs, equally fastidious. One had been thrown over their six-foot garden wall at a few weeks old and another pushed into her hand in the street with the words, 'Take it or I'll drown it.' As well as an injury from her six-foot fall, the former came with an intractable skin complaint. Margaret has spent a small fortune on veterinary treatments.

Next door to her and her family is a middle-aged man of extreme hairiness. A veritable floor mop hangs over his eyes and ears while a thick beard disappears up under the rim of his glasses and gives him the look of a wookie wearing spectacles. We only ever see him briefly, coming up for air, since he spends most of his time below. From the sounds that emerge, he appears to be constantly sawing through timber.

To our left is the kind of large old wooden boat that yacht brokers euphemistically term 'a project' which means it is quietly moldering away. With projects like this one, new owners embark on a refit full of enthusiasm and everything that is inside gets moved outside so they can sand and varnish and re-wire unimpeded.

Unfortunately, the original inspiration fades before any of this is completed and the boat ends up with rotting carpets and a marine toilet balanced on its coach house roof and a variety of wildlife breeding below decks—just like this one. At least, we assume this is where our visitor came from, through Voyager's open bathroom window. Although, if a filth-loving cockroach is going be anywhere at all, underneath a cleaning cloth in a freshly-washed and disinfected bathroom seems to be one of the least-likely places.

The cockroach is something you are always warned to keep out of your boat at all costs and something that I am irrationally revolted by. Its natural habitat is dark, dank places of festering filth and it carries the fetid stench of its lifestyle around with it as it scuttles to and fro waving two great antennae about in front of it.

Once it starts laying eggs in dark moist corners it can be difficult to get rid of. As well as scuttling about at high speed it also swims and flies. As a species it is said to be indestructible and the oldest on the planet. It has also been said of it that should man achieve the ultimate and blow himself to kingdom come, the cockroach would still be scuttling about in the radioactive debris. Imagine the sense of shock as I pick up the cloth and there one sits on the corner of the bath. I credit the ease of its demise to the fact that it was nauseous from the disinfectant fumes. From now on we keep the bathroom window screened or closed.

To the right of Voyager is another venerable hulk, although all its fittings are firmly in place. One Sunday a large extended family arrives and takes it out for the afternoon, like a monthly visit to an elderly relative being taken for a drive in the country.

The man on the boat to the right of that one we never meet. We never really see him even, just a brief glimpse a couple of times very late at night when a deck hatch opens silently, a dark shape emerges, slips off the bow and disappears into the darkness of the pontoon.

Vampires apart, it is a relaxed and friendly place. The boatyard staff is endlessly helpful, and the neighborhood policeman does his patrols in colorful beachwear on a very slow-moving jet ski with the word *Police* written on its side.

With English spoken almost everywhere it is so much easier to buy spare parts and get jobs done here. You can also buy the small things you miss much more than the larger things you have left behind, like English sausages and bacon, man-size tissues and Chicken Tikka Masala. Since our last visit, the big Safeways half a mile away has been supplemented by a small Tesco twenty seconds away as the crow flies. Checkout girls here are bilingual and juggle English and Spanish currencies with equal ease.

48

National Day

We will spend the whole of September at Sheppards Boat Yard, waiting for the return of our automatic steering from England. Not much happens. There are some lovely sunsets—one evening it is the color and texture of sugar melon with a bright light behind it—and The Rock is often a lovely shade of pink.

Two adult seagulls spend time floating around our boat trying to persuade their two large youngsters that it is time to go off and fend for themselves. This appears to be the most trying time of seagull parenthood. The youngsters duck and squirm ingratiatingly, calling piteously for sustenance. After a while one adult will fly off, unable to stand any more. The other always stays with them, but during the more prolonged wailing puts its head under water for a little peace and quiet.

The only other diversion is Royal Navy Harriers and Phantoms landing and taking off at the airstrip and flying low-level sorties over the harbor. Watching them, I wonder briefly if any of the pilots are ones that I trained.

Meanwhile we make sorties of our own, by bicycle, to stock up the galley with supplies for our Atlantic passage. One Wednesday, though, a checkout lady at the supermarket warns us that Friday is National Day and everywhere will be closed. I ask her what National Day is like.

'Everyone will be on Main Street in red and white,' she says. 'Then they look for somewhere to eat, only there isn't anywhere because they're all on Main Street in red and white. There's speeches at the naval grounds, the political bit. That's boring. Then there's things for the children to do. It's nice. Except for looking for somewhere to eat and the boring political bit.'

So, on Friday, we walk up Main Street and become absorbed into National Day. As the checkout lady had said, everywhere is shut, and everybody—or so it seems—is out on Main Street dressed in red and white, Gibraltar's national colors. You can have your face painted red and white for £1.50—every one a different design to complement your outfit—but what surprises us is the sight of so many people waving the British Union Flag with pride. Since the arrival of political correctness on England's shores its only appearance nowadays is at National Front rallies or international football games where its only purpose seems to be to goad opponents.

Here in Gibraltar it stands for national identity and continuity and self-determination as this tiny enclave struggles to retain its independence from its giant neighbor, Spain, whose demands for the The Rock to become Spanish get more insistent every year.

A little boy gives me a flag, which I take without question and carry without thinking until a middle-aged couple asks me politely to please throw it away. I had not noticed that it is not red and white but red and pale yellow, Spain's national colors. A large burger chain, they tell us, produces them to promote its outlets on the Spanish mainland, and some young Spaniards have brought quantities of them onto The Rock to distribute among the crowds. Some Gibraltarians become angry and there is the briefest of confrontations in the square.

For the rest, it is friendly, happy, smiling. Everybody, but everybody, is sporting red and white, even if it's only a red tie and a white hankie, although most have gone to great pains, not least with the most amazing hats. A woman in a wheelchair wears a red dress and a white flower. A baby in a pushchair kicks tiny feet, one in a red sock the other in white. A little girl wears the uniform of an eighteenth century British officer with bright red coat, white breeches and thigh boots. The Rock's washing lines will be red and white for days.

Nor are pets forgotten. A bow-legged English bulldog sports a coat made from a British Union flag; two white cockatoos wear red rosettes. And what looks like virtually the whole island marches down Main Street behind a banner proclaiming its desire for self-determination.

Regardless of patriotism and being under threat, it is all so amiable. Nobody elbows you, treads on your heels, or canons into you—not even the laughing youths in a conga line. The Governor makes a speech and hundreds of red and white balloons are sent aloft at 1pm. The wind takes them all to Spain. And then everybody starts looking for somewhere to eat, only there isn't anywhere because everybody is on Main Street dressed in red and white.

On the way back to the boat there is a cheerful band playing on the forecourt of the gas station at the traffic island, although the only tune that is recognizable is Happy Birthday to You. You have to cross a main intersection here to get back to Sheppards Boatyard and every time I do I think that there can be nowhere in the world where the drivers are so zealous at pedestrian crossings as Gibraltar. They *always* stop. The danger is, of course, that you get used to it, and when you leave Gibraltar you get run over.

There is a stupendous firework display after dark.

49

Warranty and Insurance

The work on our autopilot is being done under warranty and after three weeks David rings and asks when we might expect its return. The repair facility—which is in the south of England—refuses to speak to its customers direct and we have been dealing through an agent up north, in Liverpool, which prolongs the process. The message relayed from the repairer is that everybody thinks their job is a priority and we will just have to wait like everybody else. Since we are now in the last week of September, and the European sailing season is over, we wonder why we are in line behind people who will not be using their boats again until next spring. The best time to travel from Gibraltar to Madeira, however, is between May and September. And despite having arrived at Gib in the third week of August, we are now almost into October.

David seriously considers telling them to forget it, and buying a new autopilot made by another company. The only reason he does not is that the only alternative available in Gibraltar is one that had failed dismally for a friend in following seas. After five weeks of waiting, when we do finally get our unit back it is accompanied by another large bill. When queried, the answer that ultimately comes back via the agent is that it wasn't the same bit at fault as last time so we must pay all over again, plus the courier's costs.

But at last we are ready to set off. The only thing left to do now is notify our insurance broker. Yacht insurance is provided area-by-area and it is quite normal for yachtsmen to wait until they are about to set off before notifying their insurer that they are moving into a new area because the moment you do the premium goes up. And when crossing the Atlantic, the premium doubles.

WE HAD TOLD OUR insurance broker from the outset that our intention ultimately was to cross the Atlantic, so it comes as a great shock when we contact him about our departure to be told our present insurance company will not cover us for that. He then contacts a number of other insurers trying to get cover for us.

The next blow is that some of them demand a minimum crew of three for a crossing, while some want as many as four, and that anyone taken on as crew has to be as experienced as we are. This presents a number of problems. One is the prospect of having one or more total strangers sharing your confined living space for weeks. Another is the logistics of the situation. You have to carry up to twice the amount of provisions.

We are also working on the see-how-we-go, so-far-so-good principle. We have not committed ourselves to the Caribbean. If we arrive at Madeira and decide that this is as far as we want to go, we can always return to the Mediterranean, but run the risk of a really resentful crew member or two who have their hearts set on reaching the Virgin Islands.

And therein lies another problem. Once he gets to the Caribbean, the skipper of a yacht is held responsible for his crew. A ticket home must be provided to ensure that a crew member leaves when his visa expires. And if that crew member should, for instance, smash up a bar whilst in his cups, or perpetrate some other crime, the victim will be looking to that individual's skipper for compensation.

The last and perhaps most significant deterrent, is not just sharing your personal space with a total stranger, and being financially responsible for him, but the caliber of the individual involved. Horror stories are rife. Of crew who are lazy; alcoholic; who eat so much there isn't enough food left to complete the voyage; who display psychotic tendencies once out at sea; who bore you to death by talking incessantly about themselves; and the probably apocryphal but nonetheless terrifying story of a crew member whose last two skippers failed to make it to the other side alive.

Our options are limited because of a general reluctance to insure multi-hull boats anyway. Catamarans have an undeserved reputation for pitch-poling. This is because a lot of racing catamarans have come to grief through having too much canvas up in too strong a wind. Racing yachts are built for lightness and, under pressure to win, with too much sail aloft the bow goes down, the stern comes up and they capsize. And unlike monohulls, which should be—although not always are—self-righting, once a cat turns over it stays over. The answer lies in being a prudent sailor, and cruising catamaran skippers tend to be just that. Most cruising catamarans also tend to be heavier and get into trouble less easily.

Finally, with our broker unable to help us, David finds a German company which insures a lot of boats on Atlantic crossings. He contacts their British office and they tell him in a casual, almost laid-back manner, that of course they can provide cover with just the two of us as crew—solo, if that's what he wants. So *now*, we are ready to set off.

Our plan is to leave the Mediterranean through the Strait of Gibraltar and sail out into the Atlantic to Porto Santo, the second largest of The Madeira Islands, which will be our first port of call en route to the Caribbean.

The Atlantic Ocean

50

Leaving Gibraltar

Gaz of the multiple tattoos and Zapata moustache rows out in his dinghy and lifts our stern anchor for us so that we can ease our way out from between all the other stern lines and leave the pontoon. We tie up at the fuel dock where the water around us is littered with a sickly green film of diesel, assorted refuse and what looks horribly like sewage. The young attendant looks at it too and says sadly how dirty the harbor has become since the new breakwater was built on the Spanish side of the border.

'Nowadays the rubbish that comes in doesn't leave again,' he says. 'It stays until it rots onto the bottom. It used to be lush green weed down there. Now it's all black and dead.'

We fill our tank with diesel, and a can with 2-stroke for our dinghy's outboard. Then we set off on our longest-ever passage: approximately 570 miles to Porto Santo, the nearest of the islands of the Madeira archipelago. We shall need to sail wherever possible as we have a 100-mile shortfall on fuel. We leave Gibraltar with the wind in our favor and all sails up.

Our departure time has been carefully chosen to get the best tidal conditions in the Strait of Gibraltar. The millions of gallons of water which rush into the Mediterranean from the Atlantic daily, and which had carried us in so effortlessly a year ago, are inevitably pushing against us now as we navigate our way out. However, the current is presently at its weakest. We gain even greater advantage by hugging the Spanish coast, which not only keeps us out of the current's main thrust, but also away from the very busy shipping lanes.

We follow the coastline until about 4pm, by which time we are past the shipping lanes, then turn south-west and head for a point ten miles from Cap Sparte on the Moroccan coast. Two hours later we are passing Morocco and heading out to sea. We see our first gannet in months. There is now very little wind, however. So although we keep the sails up, we have to put the starboard engine on to keep our course.

Throughout the evening we pass a number of fishing boats, and Channel 16 constantly crackles with the voices of fishermen, in heavily-accented English, calling to one another, making jokes, laughing. We are surprised that they should be speaking English among themselves.

I take the first watch, at 8pm. Sometime after 10pm and a long way off the Moroccan coast some small, white, distant lights appear. They don't move and at first I assume they are fishing boats. I watch for some time and, although I cannot say why, I feel very uneasy. I can't make sense of them and though I hate to get David up before time, especially on my first watch of a long passage, I go below and wake him. He doesn't understand the lights either. The one closest to us finally reveals itself to be a buoy with a white light on it, although no buoys are shown on our chart. David changes course so that we go well to port of the end one, which is on our starboard side.

OUR ENGINE STOPS SUDDENLY, and so do we. David's immediate response, after turning off the ignition, is to hang over the stern with a torch to look for some tell-tale sign of whatever has fouled the propeller, usually discarded fishing net. We can see nothing. We go forward and hang over the bow rails, and then stare over the beams, shining a torch into the water. Eerily we appear to have stopped dead. You don't just stop dead at sea, even when your engine fails, and especially when you still have sail up.

It takes a little while in the darkness before we spot a small brown circular fishing float below the water, behind Voyager's beam on her port side, and follow a line of them forward until they disappear out of sight under her bow. It takes a little longer still to fully realize what this means.

What it means is that our boat is trapped in an enormous net.

While staring at strange lights in the distance we have been sailing into the unlit section of a drift net, possibly—we discover later—as much as 20 miles long and fifty feet deep. Voyager's bows have hit the top edge of it. With it caught around the front of her keels she has driven it ahead of her until the trailing netting has reached her props and stopped the engine. We take down the sails to prevent us being carried any further into it.

51

The Net

It is a calm night and we are in no immediate danger, but we need to free ourselves as soon as possible. We cannot see how we can do this alone. Going over the side in the dark into a huge net is not an option. The answer seems to be help from other boats, specifically those whose net it is, and who must have had this happen before. We can see the lights of several fishing boats beyond our stern, so we turn on our deck and cockpit lights to illuminate our boat and David puts out a call on the VHF. He gives our boat's name, position, says we are trapped in a net and asks for help. From that moment on, there will not be another sound from the VHF.

I make some tea and we sit in the cockpit and wait. We are ablaze with white light and stare out from its blinding glare into the surrounding darkness. After a while the lights of a fishing boat come towards us. We stand up and wait, but after traveling some distance and getting quite close to us it turns and goes away again. This happens several times. David puts out another call on the VHF giving our name, our position and asking for help to leave the net. Again we wait. After all the chatter of the earlier part of the night the silence since our first call has been unnerving.

There are things you know intuitively and things that common sense makes self-evident. But some things need to be experienced before they reach the fundamental depths of your understanding. This night is when I fully comprehend how completely alone and dependent on each other two people on a boat at sea really are.

After a while I go below and make coffee. As we sit drinking it we reassess our situation. Two hours have passed since we hit the net. No help is coming and we must decide what to do next. We can go on waiting for the boats which will come, sooner or later, to haul up the net or we can try and cut ourselves free from within the boat. The night is still calm, but if the wind should rise and the sea get rough we shall become even more entangled. If we are to free ourselves, the longer we leave it the more difficult it is likely to become. Or should we wait?

We begin to wonder about our treatment at the hands of the fishermen when they find us in their net. Fishermen are famously hostile to yachtsmen. The fate of one in Gibraltar comes to mind. His trimaran, with a gaping hole in one of its hulls, had been tied up near our berth and we had read a local newspaper article about it. A fisherman had deliberately driven his trawler at the yacht and having crippled it tried to claim salvage rights for rescuing it. The salvage aspect suddenly hits us. We had not considered the possibility of losing our boat.

The silence begins to seem ominous. Perhaps we have been foolish to wait so long.

And then with a shock I remember Annie from Humberside, in the launderette at Alicante marina last year, telling me about the night she and her husband got caught in a drift net. *It was a Saturday night, she had said, and the fishermen were all drunk. They surrounded us and fired flares at us. They were still burning when they landed on our deck. It went on for hours.*

'What day is it?' I ask.

'Saturday.'

We look at each other in the brief silence that follows. Then I go and get the boat hook and David fetches the Stanley knife.

IT TAKES BOTH OF us to drag up a section of the net until it is high enough for David to reach with the knife. It takes all my strength to hold it aloft while he cuts through it. It is hard to haul up because the boat is so tightly bound up in it, but it is even harder to cut. The rope edge, to which the nylon net is attached, and on which the circular brown floats are strung, is extremely tough. It takes us quite a while because each time we think we are free we find we are caught somewhere else.

It is some time after 1am before Voyager is finally free. What slight breeze still exists is now on the nose but for once we are grateful because it means we can put up the main and reverse away from the net under sail. We do not dare put on an engine. We know the starboard propeller at least must be entangled in the remnants of the net and unusable. We do not know if the port prop is also fouled, but it most likely is. If we try to use it, it will simply entangle it even more before that engine seizes up too.

We then turn off our deck lights and sail away, *very* slowly. There is so little wind, in fact, that at times we only manage one mile an hour. We travel south, a direction which we hope is putting us parallel with the net and wonder if we shall have to continue on this course until daylight. After a while, however, a freighter crosses our path. When we see that it meets with no opposition we assume it is beyond the end of the net and we follow its course. Then David sends me to bed.

By dawn we have covered only twelve miles. Stress and tiredness do strange things to your mental faculties and we become somewhat paranoid when a fishing boat ahead appears to be waiting for us. A man on deck eyeballs us. We stare ahead. It is probable that he is simply bemused as to why we are traveling so slowly. After a while he moves away.

His is the only vessel about, so once he is out of sight David puts on his wet suit, we heave-to and he goes under the boat to have a look. Strangely, the starboard propeller, which is the one we had been using and which we expected to be badly fouled, has very little around it. The port prop, on the other hand, is a mass of netting. I pass him a knife.

It is a long job for we have no oxygen tank aboard and he has to keep coming up for air. Then half his oxygen and quite a lot of energy are taken up in getting back down and underneath the boat again. In between times, he has to hold on with one hand and cut with the other while holding his breath.

It is also a dangerous job. We are fortunate that the sea is still calm with only a slight swell running. That swell is enough, however, to repeatedly lift Voyager and bring her banging down on David's head. On one dive he is a long time below. He has become entangled in the net and is unable to get back to the surface.

'I would like to be able to say,' he admits later, 'that I reacted with calm calculation. But my knife was slashing everywhere. My biggest surprise was that I still had all my fingers and toes when I surfaced.'

They are badly cut, however. Not by his knife, but by the nylon netting. It has also sliced through the wet suit to his skin. Eventually, however, both props are free. We are able to put on an engine and continue at normal speed.

It never fails to surprise me how unsuspected strength, sustained effort or the ability to overcome fear or fatigue materialize when a situation demands it. When the job is done, however, exhaustion kicks in. Once back on deck David is almost too tired to move. I peel him out of his wet suit, help him get dry and send him to bed. The rest of Sunday is uneventful.

52

Lost Appetites

Monday is pretty uneventful, too. An enormous moon rises at 3.22am with the sun's flush on it, turning it pearly pink. We are alone in a vast empty sea, yet the circular horizon makes it look quite small and the moon seems only a couple of miles away.

At 9am we start getting big rollers from the north which last for some hours. David loses all interest in food while I manage two dry biscuits and a cup of coffee for breakfast. By mid-day, however, I am ravenous. More than anything else I crave a bacon sandwich. I make one while David is in bed.

We are both tired and when not on watch we go and lie down. When you sleep in three-and-a-half hour shifts it takes a while to get in your eight hours. Even then, sleep which is disturbed every few hours is not as refreshing as a continuous night's rest. We also lost sleep through the drift net and it is vital to recover our energy as soon as possible. Should we have another emergency we will need to be as fresh as possible to cope with it.

After eating my bacon sandwich I open all the hatches and wash the frying pan so as not to turn David green when he gets up. I follow the sandwich with a slice of date and walnut cake and feel confident that I have gained my sea legs. By evening, however, another bout of rollers puts paid to any plans for a chicken pasta dinner. We have half a bread roll each with honey on it, and a cup of tea. Not surprisingly, you often end a long passage thinner than when you set out.

The sun sets without much fanfare, but when it gets dark the stars are incredible. There is also phosphorescence on the water. I look down from the helm and watch it roll off our bow-wave and tumble down the side of the boat. It is evanescent. At the very moment that the sparkling silver lights appear, so they disappear, vanishing before you can fully focus on them and all you can do is let your eyes go slack and simply absorb the radiance.

The only vessels we see all day are two tankers. Inevitably the three of us are on a collision course, but courses get changed and we pass safely. We see no other craft beyond a light on the horizon just before midnight.

53

Sleep Deprivation

On Tuesday I do the 3-6.30am watch again. The stars are very bright, but the sea is misty and the radar is on. The moon rises at 4.37 behind our stern, pearly pink again like yesterday. Sometime later a light appears on the horizon directly behind us and I assume it is another tanker, although it does not appear on the radar.

As the light gets larger, however, it gets higher like the masthead light of an approaching yacht. It has still not appeared on the radar, however, and I become anxious that if they are not appearing on *our* screen, we may not be visible on theirs. And although many leisure boats do not have radar, this one must, since judging by the speed that the light is gaining on us it is a large and very powerful yacht. It is exactly on our course so I put on our cockpit light to make sure that we can be clearly seen.

The light behind us keeps rising until it is so high that it finally dawns on me what I have been watching all this time and I switch off our cockpit light. It is not the masthead light of a super yacht that we have behind us. It is the Morning Star. For the past half hour or so I have been signaling a warning of our presence to the planet Venus.

Throughout the day large Atlantic rollers from the north continue to pummel our starboard beam. Just moving about the boat becomes an effort, and it is not restful to the stomach. Our queasiness passes, however, and we resume light but regular meals. I still see very little of David except at mealtimes. We are both so tired that one of us still sleeps while the other watches, even through the day. I really do not know how lone sailors manage. And not just from tiredness either.

A boat makes noises and at night, alone on watch, the imagination takes over. At least, mine does. I begin thinking of The Fog again when passing through the unlit galley there is a groan like a soul in torment. I actually cry out, it startles me so much, and feel really foolish when I discover it is the handle of a mug rubbing on a cup hook close to my ear.

Out in the cockpit I glimpse something hunched on the side deck in the blackness and recoil in horror. It is only our lifebuoy. After several hours of staring out into a bouncing sea, I begin to see lights that are not there. In truth, there is *nothing* out here now but sea and sky and us. I have never before felt so exposed to the universe.

As I begin to fall asleep, after my watch, I hear a conversation above my head between a man and a woman and assume David is listening to World Service in the cockpit.

'No,' he says later. 'And if I had been, I'd have used the earphones so as not to keep you awake.'

He had actually been sitting at the chart table at the time, reading a yachting magazine article about the Mini Transat Race. It is for single sailors in 21-foot yachts capable of 23mph. Their boats are so stripped out for speed that the galley is a kettle welded onto a Primus stove and they live on Pot Noodles. Apparently the worst thing is sleep deprivation, to the point where one participant rang up his shore-based team to say that he had just been overtaken by a motorcycle.

There was a TV program last winter about clinical research into sleep in which researchers woke up volunteers before or during their rapid-eye-movement (REM) or dreaming stage. Deprived of this essential phase over several nights, the volunteers began to compensate by dreaming while awake. I begin to do this now. While sitting upright with my eyes open and to all appearances wide awake I will verbalize the end of a dream I am having and wake to find a startled David saying, '*What* did you say?'

So I can perfectly empathize with a lone sailor who thinks he has just been overtaken by a motorbike.

When David takes over the watch from me at breakfast time he says he has also started hearing voices in the cockpit above his head. But when I ask him what they said he says they were talking just that bit too quietly for him to make out individual words. The wind has risen considerably this morning. When I settle into the helmsman's chair with my cereal bowl the cornflakes keep blowing off the spoon.

AROUND 3PM TWO BATTERED old cargo ships appear to port. One is on a course which causes us no problems. The other is on a collision course with us. There are a couple of rules of the sea involved here. Firstly, power gives way to sail. Secondly, the vessel that can turn to starboard to avoid a collision should do so.

It soon becomes apparent that the cargo boat is not interested in either of them, so David puts on both engines and accelerates out of its way. As the vessel passes close behind us we can see that there is no-one on the bridge keeping a lookout. In fact, apart from the ship's small, round-faced cook, who emerges from the wheelhouse with one arm full of cabbages and cheerfully waves the other at us, I doubt whether anyone has noticed we are even there.

In the meantime, we have both recovered our energy today and this evening feel strong enough to finally tackle chicken pasta. I stand the chicken, now well past its best-before date, on the draining board to air and take the vegetables up into the cockpit. It is far nicer to prepare them sitting outside than standing in a galley with malodorous chicken. I also discover the aerodynamics of the cockpit while peeling the garlic. The breeze catches the paper-thin skin and it loops-the-loop before settling into the corners of the cockpit sole. One piece even flies out beyond the stern but turns round and comes back in again to join the rest. At least it explains why so much debris gathers in the cockpit's corners.

Sunset tonight is invisible because of cloud and the sky becomes threatening, especially in the direction that we are heading. The night is very dark and the phosphorous startlingly bright. Previously it has appeared only around the boat. Now it also lights the tops of breaking waves some distance away, creating long pale strips that resemble a boat's hull rushing towards us. Elsewhere it glitters like navigation lights in the distance, only to vanish and reappear somewhere else. Combined with the sea banging against our hull, and the wind suddenly soaring and just as suddenly dropping, it makes for a jittery night.

54

Plodding On

It is four o'clock on Wednesday morning and still very dark. I have eye-balled a white light for an hour. It seems to be forever off our port beam. Beyond a certain distance and depending on the atmosphere, color disappears. At night it is only a vessel's red and green navigation lights which tell you in which direction it is traveling—at you or away from you. At present, color is not visible above seven miles. Finally I am able to identify a red light. It tells me the vessel will go behind and away from us, but it does so incredibly slowly.

The wind is erratic, oscillating between 15 and 25mph. We are under sail but have the port engine on idle to power the radar. Our radar fairly sucks up juice and flat batteries at sea would cause huge problems. Meanwhile, it has become cold and I am huddled in my foul weather jacket. There are a few stars directly above now, but it is still extremely dark. The moon is not due until around six this morning but I will be unable to see it, or the Morning Star, because of all this cloud.

By mid-morning, however, it looks as if the words *The Simpsons* should appear through the rows of white fluffy clouds. Behind them the sky is every conceivable shade of blue, from palest gold-tinted aquamarine at the horizon to a deep, glowing cobalt directly overhead. A super-tanker, *enormous*, crosses our path, David checks the engine oil and we try unsuccessfully again today to hear the weather forecast broadcast by French Radio. The woman currently reading it has a breathy voice more suited to seduction, or the cajoling of small children, than a mariner with an ear clamped to a crackling receiver. Not that it really makes much difference to us at present. With nothing but sea and sky between departure and arrival, all you can do is keep plodding on. It would have been comforting, however, to have been able to tune into that sonorous baritone voice and hear once again, *'Visibilita: discreto. Vento: diminuzione. Mare: poco mosso.'*

We have the most delicious meal of our lives tonight: corned beef and fresh vegetables with melting butter and freshly-ground black pepper. I don't know why it tastes so good, but it does.

55

Blobs in the Night

It is just after midnight, a few minutes into Thursday and the start of our sixth day at sea, when David gets me out of bed so that we can both stare at a number of large dappled blobs on the radar screen. I turn bemused sleepy eyes towards him.

'I don't know,' he says helplessly. 'I've never seen anything like it before.'

Nor have I. Boats don't look like this on a radar screen. Depending on size they appear either as a small dot or a modest dash. These things are large blobs, flat at the bottom and rounded at the top, like old-fashioned haystacks except that by measuring them against the rings of the radar screen they each appear to be around a mile wide.

'I'm bewildered,' says David. 'There are no islands out here and they're too big for whales. I'm sorry to get you up but I need another pair of eyes.'

Mine can't help noticing that whatever these things are, we appear to be sailing straight at one of them. I point this out to him.

'I've already changed course three times to avoid it,' he says patiently. 'But every time I look at the screen we're heading directly for it again.'

I go outside and stare into the blackness. It is a waste of time. It is so dark that the only thing you could possibly have seen out here would have been a light, only there is none. David follows me outside and climbs up into the helmsman's chair to change course again. By now he is more than half-convinced that there is something wrong with our steering. He remains at the controls, with nothing ahead of him but impenetrable darkness.

I go back inside to the chart table and stare at the radar screen again. But with one of us watching the screen and the other the compass it soon becomes apparent that the blobs are not static, as originally thought, but moving very slowly. We are not drifting into them, but they into us.

And then, bathed in the eerie green light of the radar screen, I see another blob appear. Only this one is directly behind our stern and gaining on us quite quickly. Until now, all our attention has been focused in front of us. As one, we go and stare out over our stern. After a few moments there is a tiny spatter of water against our faces, although there is no accompanying sound or disturbance to the sea around us. We stand side-by-side in a black night in a black sea surrounded by some threat but not knowing what it is.

Then another little spatter of water hits us, a little harder this time, and on the very edge of my hearing I can just detect a faint, erratic, whizzing sound and finally know what it is that's creeping up behind us. A squall: a very strong wind, usually containing rain or snow, traveling so fast that it can pass over you in only minutes but so violent that it can do considerable damage.

We have experienced many before, but always in daylight when you can see their black cloud and thick column of rain approaching from miles away. We have never been caught in one at night before. And in our inexperience we had not realized that you could see weather on a radar screen.

A squall is one of the ways a yacht can lose its mast, or even a crew member, at night. Blithely sailing along with its sails filled by a moderate wind, it is suddenly hit by a very strong one. A squall is at its most dangerous when, as sometimes happens, it brings with it a sudden change of wind direction. This can cause the boom to gybe and hurl overboard any crewman unfortunate enough to be in its way; or put so much stress on a mast under full sail that it is torn away from its mountings. When a mast carrying full sail goes overboard, with its shrouds, fore and back stays still attached to the deck, the drag on the hull is so great that it can capsize the yacht unless the crew is able to cut away the rigging in time.

We do not simply have one squall threatening us, though, we are surrounded by them. Now we know what they are, however, we reef the sails and use the radar to avoid them. It is like fairground dodgems only instead of a bump when one gets too close to us, we get a drenching from the flying rain at its outer edges.

Buffeted, wet, tired but intact, ultimately we sail through them and leave them behind. Conditions gradually return to what they were before—dry, cloudy and very dark—until around 2.30am when the sky clears suddenly and becomes brilliant with stars. I think that in the right circumstances it must be possible to get drunk on stars. Certainly, after a dark and stressful night, I am pleasantly tipsy on these.

The Madeira Islands

56

Porto Santo

Just after dawn we spot three peaks in the distance ahead of us. It is Porto Santo. Although the modern GPS is so accurate that it makes navigation easy these days, it is still exciting to have reached a very small island out in the Atlantic Ocean. We always knew we would find it, but it is still a relief that we have, and that the three of us are still in one piece. There is also a sort of thrill, a sense of the unknown, perhaps not unlike the first explorers felt, but without their relief at not having fallen off the edge of the world. Although it is doubtful whether they did, in fact, believe this is what might happen to them. People in the past were often far more intelligent, sophisticated and well-educated than some of our history books give them credit for.

One thing we do know for certain is that we have been traveling in the wake of the first recorded explorers, in particular two Portuguese sailors called Zarco and Teixeira. They were part of Henry the Navigator's grand plan and in 1418 were heading for Africa when they were driven off course by a gale. They eventually found shelter in the lee of a small, unknown island which in gratitude they called Porto Santo—Holy Port.

It was the first of the Atlantic Islands to be discovered. Portugal colonized it and its first governor was a minor nobleman remembered nowadays as Christopher Columbus's father-in-law. And we know we are in Portuguese territory again when we finally pass the lighthouse off the south-eastern tip of the island. It is like a Mediterranean villa with trees planted around it—a little version of the one to the west of Portugal's Lagos.

One of the surprising things about traveling by yacht is the length of time that passes between that first sight of land and actually arriving. It seems to take for*ever*. And, indeed, it is five and a half hours between spotting Porto Santo's three volcanic peaks and dropping our anchor off that same pristine, six-mile-long beach where Zarco and Teixeira found shelter in 1418.

Gibraltar mud rises from our anchor and chain, and lies like scum on the crystal clear water.

THIS CROSSING HAS BEEN our first experience of being any great distance from land. The Balearics and Sardinia had been but a day or so away. Even the Bay of Biscay had taken us only two and a half days to cross. A concern about the distances involved in Atlantic crossings is that, should an emergency occur, two people might not be enough to handle it. However, we have done a six-day passage, covered 576 miles, weathered a crisis, recovered our energy reasonably quickly and completed the voyage safely. We get out the cockpit cushions, open a bottle of wine and put up our feet.

'You know,' says David, 'I finally feel like a real blue water cruiser.'

I do, too. It is some years since I received my Competent Crew certificate at the end of a one-week sailing course in Wales, but only now do I feel worthy of the title. We lean back against the cushions and take stock. In particular, how are we? That had, after all, been our priority: to improve our health and quality of life.

David is thirty pounds lighter than when we set out last year. It is weight he has wanted to lose for decades but which had proved resistant, buttressed by an office desk and long-distance business travel. The early improvement he had experienced in his respiratory system, thanks to a reduction of allergens from living on water, has also been maintained. In short, he is slimmer, fitter and healthier than he has been since his twenties.

I am fitter and stronger than I have been since my twenties too, thanks to the simple daily exercise required by life aboard. Just the basic tasks of sailing, simple maintenance, exploring each new place we visit, or simply walking the mile or so to a supermarket or launderette. And there are, of course, the added health benefits of being a non-smoker.

Life has become simpler, too. We now own neither house nor car and have on board only those material possessions which fulfill our basic needs. It is surprising, and surprisingly satisfying, to discover just how little you really need.

Our diet has also become simpler thanks to a gentler climate and the absence of processed foods. Fresh fruit and vegetables. Chicken and fish, simply cooked. Olive oil. Tomatoes. A few herbs. Fresh crusty bread. Local cheeses with fresh olives. A glass of wine. *And thou*, as a Persian poet wrote so memorably.

In short, we have become relaxed and happy in our new life, while at the same time maintaining an easy but constant vigilance in regard to what is happening to our boat and the weather, in planning voyages, gathering vital information for them, and doing all those things which are not only necessary for our enjoyment but essential to our safety. And ultimately, of course, our survival. Because, as the drift net and the night squalls proved, *in extremis* there is nobody out there to save you but yourselves. Knowing that, and accepting it, makes you strong.

So when David asks, 'Shall we carry on to the Caribbean?' the answer is unhesitatingly,

'Yes.'

Glossary

Anti-fouling – paint put on the hull below the water line to deter marine vegetation and shellfish which reduce the speed of a boat.

Autopilot – device to hold the boat on a set course automatically.

Backstays, forestays, and shrouds – multi-strand, stainless-steel cables which support the mast.

Beam – the widest part of the hull, usually towards the centre of the boat.

Beaufort Wind Force Scale - created in 1805 by Sir Francis Beaufort, a British naval officer and hydrographer, before instruments were available. The scale begins with Force 1 – Light Airs at 1-3mph and rises to Force 12 – Hurricane at 73+mph. Those used in this book are Force 6 (Strong Breeze 25-31mph); Near Gale Force 7 (32-38mph); Gale Force 8 (39-46mph); and Strong Gale Force 9 (47-54mph).

Blue water cruising – long distance ocean cruising.

Boom – a hinged beam attached to the mast which holds the bottom of the main sail and allows it to be set in various positions to catch the wind.

Car boot sale – British equivalent of a yard sale, only out of a car's trunk.

Davits – two small cranes to lift and hold a dinghy, usually at a boat's stern.

Gash bag – all trash on board is bagged and taken ashore for appropriate disposal.

Gelcoat – the hard shiny outer layer covering the fiberglass from which the boat is made.

Genoa – the large sail in front of our mast.

GPS – global positioning system which tells you where you are now, what course to follow to reach your destination, and other essential data.

Hard – abr. for hard standing, when a boat is lifted out of the water to allow work to be done on its hull.

Lazy line – when a boat is berthed bows-on, it is held off the quay or pontoon by a lazy line, a mooring rope which is fixed to the seabed at one end and tied to the boat's stern cleat at the other.

Line (or shore line) – the rope used to tie a boat to the shore.

Log – (1) a speedometer. (2) a manual record which in our case includes weather, location, direction, events.

Main sail – the large sail behind the mast.

Navtex – receiver for international weather forecasts in English, either on a screen or as a print out.

Outhaul – rope used to haul out a sail.

Painter – a rope attached to the bow of a dinghy, used for tying it up.

Phoenicians – formidable sailors and traders of the first and second millennium BC whose homeland was a narrow strip of land along the eastern Mediterranean coast which is now modern Lebanon plus parts of Syria and Israel and which once included the biblical cities of Sidon and Tyre.

Port – left-hand side of vessel looking forward.

Red ensign – the official flag for British Merchant Navy ships and British leisure boats.

RIB – rigid inflatable boat; a high-speed rubber dinghy with a glass fiber bottom.

Sheets – ropes used to control a sail.

Starboard – right-hand side of vessel looking forward.

Squall – sudden increase in wind-speed, often accompanied by brief but heavy precipitation.

Lightning Source UK Ltd.
Milton Keynes UK
171670UK00002B/48/P